Number 155
Fall 2017

New Directions for Evaluation

Paul R. Brandon
Editor-in-Chief

Pedagogy of Evaluation

Michael Quinn Patton
Editor

Pedagogy of Evaluation
Michael Quinn Patton (ed.)
New Directions for Evaluation, no. 155
Editor-in-Chief: *Paul R. Brandon*

New Directions for Evaluation, (ISSN 1097-6736; Online ISSN: 1534-875X), is published quarterly on behalf of the American Evaluation Association by Wiley Subscription Services, Inc., a Wiley Company, 111 River St., Hoboken, NJ 07030-5774 USA.
Postmaster: Send all address changes to *New Directions for Evaluation*, John Wiley & Sons Inc., C/O The Sheridan Press, PO Box 465, Hanover, PA 17331 USA.

Information for subscribers
New Directions for Evaluation is published in 4 issues per year. Institutional subscription prices for 2017 are:
Print & Online: US$484 (US), US$538 (Canada & Mexico), US$584 (Rest of World), €381 (Europe), £304 (UK). Prices are exclusive of tax. Asia-Pacific GST, Canadian GST/HST and European VAT will be applied at the appropriate rates. For more information on current tax rates, please go to www.wileyonlinelibrary.com/tax-vat. The price includes online access to the current and all online back-files to January 1st 2013, where available. For other pricing options, including access information and terms and conditions, please visit www.wileyonlinelibrary.com/access.

Delivery Terms and Legal Title
Where the subscription price includes print issues and delivery is to the recipient's address, delivery terms are **Delivered at Place (DAP)**; the recipient is responsible for paying any import duty or taxes. Title to all issues transfers FOB our shipping point, freight prepaid. We will endeavour to fulfil claims for missing or damaged copies within six months of publication, within our reasonable discretion and subject to availability.

Back issues: Single issues from current and recent volumes are available at the current single issue price from cs-journals@wiley.com.

Disclaimer
The Publisher, the American Evaluation Association and Editors cannot be held responsible for errors or any consequences arising from the use of information contained in this journal; the views and opinions expressed do not necessarily reflect those of the Publisher, the American Evaluation Association and Editors, neither does the publication of advertisements constitute any endorsement by the Publisher, the American Evaluation Association and Editors of the products advertised.

Publisher: New Directions for Evaluation is published by Wiley Periodicals, Inc., 350 Main St., Malden, MA 02148-5020.

Journal Customer Services: For ordering information, claims and any enquiry concerning your journal subscription please go to www.wileycustomerhelp.com/ask or contact your nearest office.
Americas: Email: cs-journals@wiley.com; Tel: +1 781 388 8598 or +1 800 835 6770 (toll free in the USA & Canada).
Europe, Middle East and Africa: Email: cs-journals@wiley.com; Tel: +44 (0) 1865 778315.
Asia Pacific: Email: cs-journals@wiley.com; Tel: +65 6511 8000.
Japan: For Japanese speaking support, Email: cs-japan@wiley.com.
Visit our Online Customer Help available in 7 languages at www.wileycustomerhelp.com/ask

Production Editor: Meghanjali Singh (email: mesingh@wiley.com).

Wiley's Corporate Citizenship initiative seeks to address the environmental, social, economic, and ethical challenges faced in our business and which are important to our diverse stakeholder groups. Since launching the initiative, we have focused on sharing our content with those in need, enhancing community philanthropy, reducing our carbon impact, creating global guidelines and best practices for paper use, establishing a vendor code of ethics, and engaging our colleagues and other stakeholders in our efforts. Follow our progress at www.wiley.com/go/citizenship

View this journal online at wileyonlinelibrary.com/journal/ev

Wiley is a founding member of the UN-backed HINARI, AGORA, and OARE initiatives. They are now collectively known as Research4Life, making online scientific content available free or at nominal cost to researchers in developing countries. Please visit Wiley's Content Access - Corporate Citizenship site: http://www.wiley.com/WileyCDA/Section/id-390082.html

Printed in the USA by The Sheridan Group.

Address for Editorial Correspondence: Editor-in-chief, Paul R. Brandon, New Directions for Evaluation, Email: brandon@hawaii.edu

Abstracting and Indexing Services
The Journal is indexed by Academic Search Alumni Edition (EBSCO Publishing); Education Research Complete (EBSCO Publishing); Higher Education Abstracts (Claremont Graduate University); SCOPUS (Elsevier); Social Services Abstracts (ProQuest); Sociological Abstracts (ProQuest); Worldwide Political Sciences Abstracts (ProQuest).

Cover design: Wiley
Cover Images: © Lava 4 images | Shutterstock

For submission instructions, subscription and all other information visit: wileyonlinelibrary.com/journal/ev

Editorial Policy and Procedures

New Directions for Evaluation, a quarterly sourcebook, is an official publication of the American Evaluation Association. The journal publishes works on all aspects of evaluation, with an emphasis on presenting timely and thoughtful reflections on leading-edge issues of evaluation theory, practice, methods, the profession, and the organizational, cultural, and societal context within which evaluation occurs. Each issue of the journal is devoted to a single topic, with contributions solicited, organized, reviewed, and edited by one or more guest editors.

The editor-in-chief is seeking proposals for journal issues from around the globe about topics new to the journal (although topics discussed in the past can be revisited). A diversity of perspectives and creative bridges between evaluation and other disciplines, as well as chapters reporting original empirical research on evaluation, are encouraged. A wide range of topics and substantive domains are appropriate for publication, including evaluative endeavors other than program evaluation; however, the proposed topic must be of interest to a broad evaluation audience.

Journal issues may take any of several forms. Typically they are presented as a series of related chapters, but they might also be presented as a debate; an account, with critique and commentary, of an exemplary evaluation; a feature-length article followed by brief critical commentaries; or perhaps another form proposed by guest editors.

Submitted proposals must follow the format found via the Association's website at http://www.eval.org/Publications/NDE.asp. Proposals are sent to members of the journal's Editorial Advisory Board and to relevant substantive experts for single-blind peer review. The process may result in acceptance, a recommendation to revise and resubmit, or rejection. The journal does not consider or publish unsolicited single manuscripts.

Before submitting proposals, all parties are asked to contact the editor-in-chief, who is committed to working constructively with potential guest editors to help them develop acceptable proposals. For additional information about the journal, see the "Statement of the Editor-in-Chief" in the Spring 2013 issue (No. 137).

Paul R. Brandon, Editor-in-Chief
University of Hawai'i at Mānoa
College of Education
1776 University Avenue
Castle Memorial Hall, Rm. 118
Honolulu, HI 968222463
e-mail: nde@eval.org

Contents

Part 3. Freire's Current Evaluation Influence Illustrated

Statement of the Co Editors-in-Chief

This issue marks the transition of the Editor-in-Chief (EIC) role from Paul Brandon to the new Co-Editors, Leslie Fierro and Todd Franke. Readers who have taken advantage of the content of *New Directions for Evaluation* (*NDE*) in previous years will know that Paul has served as an exceptional EIC. We are deeply honored that AEA has entrusted us with this important role, and it is our hope that we can continue to uphold the standards Paul employed during his tenure and to dedicate ourselves as fully as he has to producing issues that are informative to our field. Over the past seven months, Paul has patiently mentored us through the processes involved in the EIC role, without his coaching we would be entering a great unknown, instead we feel as well prepared as one possibly can for such a journey.

In addition to Paul's tutelage, we will be well supported by our 24-member Editorial Board some of whom are continuing their tenure as Board members and others who are joining anew. We selected our Editorial Board with the intention of including voices from across our discipline—from individuals who reside in academia instructing students, conducting research on evaluation, and practicing evaluation to others who have full-time roles as internal or external evaluators within independent consulting or large commercial firms, foundations, and the government, building evaluation capacity and conducting evaluations. Collectively with our Editorial Board we have experienced evaluation across a broad range of substantive areas including but not limited to—medicine, public health, education, public administration, social work, and environment. It is our expectation that this diversity of lenses will help facilitate the publication of *NDE* issues that will contribute to the growth of our field.

We have a passion for promoting, sustaining, and actively engaging in collaborative processes to build the field of evaluation and feel that *NDE* plays an incredibly important role in this process. With this in mind, we have several focal points as the incoming co-EICs. First, we encourage potential guest editors to develop proposals that embrace, highlight, and aim to find creative solutions to the challenges we experience as evaluation practitioners. It is important to us, and we believe the field more generally, that we find better ways to connect research, theory, and practice, and it is our hope that some of the *NDE* issues published during our tenure will aim to thoughtfully connect these three domains. Second, evaluation is conducted in contexts that reflect a dynamic interplay of systems ranging from the individual to societal which can interlock well or be out of alignment at any point in time. We live in a time that seems to have become increasingly complex, divisive, and in some ways unstable, indicating a potential imbalance in these systems. Proposals for issues that highlight how evaluation can meaningfully contribute to promoting the advancement of society, social betterment, and addressing the issues of our time are strongly encouraged. Third, the field of evaluation has a slight tendency toward being insular. In reviewing the existing literature in our field, we often find that we cite each other and do not always draw upon relevant and substantial bodies of work that exist in other disciplines. Future directions for our field may come from conversations, thought experiments, and research that integrates perspectives and bodies of scholarship from evaluation and beyond (e.g., cognitive psychology, business administration, public policy, arts and humanities). Finally, we will adopt one of the aims that Paul Brandon put forth in 2013, reporting on high-quality research on evaluation. Building upon our previous point, such research may come from within the field of evaluation itself, but it may also come from collaborations between evaluation scholars and those outside of our discipline, or from other disciplines altogether.

NEW DIRECTIONS FOR EVALUATION, no. 155, Fall 2017 © 2017 Wiley Periodicals, Inc., and the American Evaluation Association. Published online in Wiley Online Library (wileyonlinelibrary.com) • DOI: 10.1002/ev.20271

We look forward to working with the Editorial Board and guest editors to continue producing insightful issues that push our field forward, as well as seeing all of you at AEA this November in Washington, DC. For those of you considering topics for potential issues, please do not hesitate to reach out to us. We will be hosting several sessions via webinars and in-person at upcoming conferences describing the process for submitting to the journal and general manuscript preparation. For additional information on the process for submitting full proposals, please visit: http://www.eval.org/p/cm/ld/fid=48.

Leslie A. Fierro, Ph.D., MPH
Assistant Clinical Professor
of Evaluation
Claremont Graduate University
Division of Organizational
and Behavioral Sciences
Leslie.Fierro@cgu.edu

Todd Michael Franke, Ph.D., MSW
Professor
UCLA
Department of Social Welfare
tfranke@g.ucla.edu

NEW DIRECTIONS FOR EVALUATION • DOI: 10.1002/ev

EDITOR'S NOTES

P edagogy is the study of teaching. *Pedagogy of evaluation* entails examining how and what evaluation teaches. There is no singular or monolithic pedagogy of evaluation. Embedded in different evaluation approaches are varying assumptions, values, premises, priorities, and sense-making processes. Those who participate in an evaluation are experiencing sometimes explicit, more often implicit and tacit, pedagogical principles. Evaluation invites stakeholders involved to see the world in a certain way, to make sense of what is being evaluated through a particular lens, to make judgments based on certain kinds of evidence and values.

This volume is inspired by and builds on the works of Paulo Freire, especially his classic, *Pedagogy of the Oppressed* (1970/2000). His other books include *Pedagogy of Indignation, Pedagogy of Hope, Pedagogy of Freedom* (2001), *Ecopedagogy*, and *Critical Pedagogy*.

Those evaluation approaches that have been most influenced by Freirean pedagogy and share Freirean values, modes of engagement, and desired outcomes are social justice-focused evaluations, democratic deliberative evaluation, empowerment evaluation, feminist evaluation, transformative evaluation, and critical systems evaluation. Evaluation's actual and potential role in examining the effects and implications of inequality is a core concern of the social justice perspective in evaluation (House, 1990, 2014; Rosenstein & Syna, 2015; Sirotnik, 1990). Other evaluation approaches value, teach, and strive for different results; that is, they are based on other pedagogical premises and principles.

The larger understanding that Freire's work reminds us of is that all evaluation approaches constitute a pedagogy of some kind. All evaluation teaches something. What is taught and how it is taught varies, but evaluation is inherently and predominantly a pedagogical interaction. Freire understood and taught us that all interactions between and among people are pedagogical; something is always being taught, conveyed, and proselytized. This volume invites you to use Freire's works to reflect on your pedagogy of evaluation. The volume is organized in three parts:

Part 1. Contemporaries of Paulo Freire present his pedagogy
Part 2. Pedagogical principles of evaluation derived from Freire
Part 3. Freire's current evaluation influence illustrated

Who was Paulo Freire, what did he contribute, and why is his pedagogy relevant to evaluation today?

Freire's strategy of considering knowledge a power resource has been rediscovered in the context of the "knowledge society" (Neirotti, 2012,

NEW DIRECTIONS FOR EVALUATION, no. 155, Fall 2017 © 2017 Wiley Periodicals, Inc., and the American Evaluation Association. Published online in Wiley Online Library (wileyonlinelibrary.com) • DOI: 10.1002/ev.20254

p. 12). Acknowledging and elevating Pablo Freire's thought and work as it applies to evaluation is especially appropriate as the field of evaluation has become increasing international in perspective and global in practice. The International Year of Evaluation in 2015 marked a major milestone in evaluation's development and recognition, and the evaluation attention being paid to the new Sustainability Development Goals builds on that momentum. Many only know about Freire's contribution to developing a transformative method for teaching illiterates in Latin America many years ago. A *New Directions for Evaluation* volume on *Evaluation Voices from Latin America* noted:

> Participation as a concept was elicited by developments in the 1970s as a response to a discourse focused on an increase in production and productivity and the adoption of new technologies. It was argued that those living in poverty, including indigenous (original) peoples, had to be the focus of development, valuing their knowledge. The discourse was framed by thinkers and social leaders like the Brazilian Paulo Freire, whose pedagogical approach to community engagement sought to "politically conscientize" marginalized groups and provoke citizen agency. His thoughts... massively influenced schooling and led to a uniquely Latin American approach to street-level action research. (Kushner & Rotondo, 2012, p. 1)

At a time when the gap between rich and poor is growing, both in industrialized countries and globally, it is illuminative to look at how the pedagogy of the oppressed and the pedagogy of certain evaluation approaches intersect.

Freire's Background and Life Experiences Shaped His Pedagogical Ideas

He was born in Brazil in 1921 at a time of world economic crisis in which he experienced hunger and poverty at a young age. He recalled: "I didn't understand anything because of my hunger. I wasn't dumb. It wasn't lack of interest. My social condition didn't allow me to have an education. Experience showed me the relationship between social class and knowledge" (quoted in Gadotti, 1994, p. 13). Because Freire lived among poor rural families and laborers, he gained a deep understanding of their lives and of the effects of socio-economics on education. Freire became a grammar teacher while still in high school, where he began developing a dialogic approach to education in which he strived to understand students' expectations and experiences. He became an activist working for a more democratic and universal approach to education in Brazil.

In 1964, Freire was imprisoned in Brazil for 70 days as a traitor. He was subsequently exiled and worked in Chile for 5 years in the Christian Democratic Agrarian Reform Movement. In 1967 he published his first book,

Education as the Practice of Freedom, bringing him acclaim and a position as visiting professor at Harvard. In 1968, while in exile, he wrote his famous *Pedagogy of the Oppressed*, published initially in Spanish and English in 1970, and subsequently in 17 languages, but not in Brazil until 1974.

Freire was recruited to Geneva in 1970, where he worked for 10 years as a special educational advisor to the World Congress of Churches. In that capacity he traveled worldwide helping countries to implement popular education and literacy reforms (Freire returned to Brazil in 1979 after being granted amnesty. He then became Secretary of Education in São Paulo, worked in universities and social organizations, and wrote until his death in 1997.

The work and lives of Paulo Freire, Ivan Illich, Camilo Torres, and Orlando Fals Borja, sharing similar values and principles, inspired liberation theology, participatory action research (PAR), and radical perspectives on learning and education (Fals-Borda & Rahman, 1991), and "in Freire's case the establishment of an entire field of critical pedagogy throughout North America" (Kahn & Kellner, 2007, p. 431). Another example of Freire's lasting influence is *Reflect*, an innovative approach to adult learning and social change that fuses the theories of Freire with participatory methodologies. It was developed in the 1990s through pilot projects in Bangladesh, Uganda, and El Salvador and is now used by over 500 organizations in over 70 countries worldwide (http://www.reflect-action.org/).

Freire's Relevance Today and Looking Forward

The idea for this volume emerged in the summer of 2014, when the Roberto Marinho Foundation (Fundação Roberto Marinho) hosted an evaluation presentation on developmental evaluation (Patton, 2011). Discussion ensued about Freirean principles. Vilma Guimarães and Thereza Penna Firme, authors of chapters in this volume, were part of that conversation and the first to envision this volume. Thomaz Chianca, another chapter author in that conversation, was a leader in forming the Brazilian Network for Monitoring and Evaluation. Indeed, four of the six chapters are by Brazilians with special knowledge of and ties to Freire.

I read Freire's *Pedagogy of the Oppressed* in graduate school in a Sociology of Development seminar at the University of Wisconsin, Madison. Vietnam War protests dominated the campus. I had just returned from Peace Corps service working with subsistence farmers in Burkina Faso. The professors teaching development had never lived among the poor and their lack of experience, and their concomitant ignorance, were alienating. The academic literature on development felt far removed from the realities of peasant life. Freire was the standout exception. His writing was deeply grounded in direct experiences with people in poverty. Oppression was not an abstraction for him. It was his lived experience. His *Pedagogy of the Oppressed* elevated the poor and honored their capacity for transformation.

Fast forward to today—Freirean principles, though articulated nearly 50 years ago, offer and affirm future directions for both development and, to the point here, evaluation. The principles remain fresh and timely, and dare I say, *new*—new in the sense that they remain far from realization, especially as an integrated whole. Given that premise, Chapter 3, written by this editor, reviews the significance and influence of Freire's works and their relevance for and impact on evaluation. That analysis generated 10 pedagogical principles I've extracted from Freire's writings and the Brazilian contributions in this volume. I explain each principle and its relevance for a critical pedagogy of evaluation. Now to an overview of this volume.

Part 1: Fresh Perspectives

This volume offers evaluators an opportunity to meet people who bring experiences and perspectives we don't regularly encounter. The Brazilian authors of these chapters knew and worked with Paulo Freire. They are sharing their experiences and insights about the implications for evaluation of Freire's pedagogy. Because who they are matters for what they have to say, I want to provide deeper than usual introductions. Their reflections are original for this volume and have never been pulled together in one place before. Part 1 contains two chapters.

Chapter 1, "The Global Influence of Freire's Pedagogy," is written by Dr. Moacir Gadotti, professor of education at the University of São Paulo and director of the Instituto Paulo Freire in São Paulo. We are deeply honored to have Dr. Gadotti contribute to this volume. He was one of Freire's closest collaborators after Freire's return to Brazil from exile. They worked together for almost 20 years. He was Chief of Cabinet when Paulo Freire was Secretary of Education of the city of Sao Paulo. His book, *Reading Paulo Freire: His Life and Work*, offers important insights into Freire's contributions. In this chapter, written especially for *New Directions for Evaluation*, Dr. Gadotti introduces a new generation of evaluators to Freire and reminds those of us who discovered him long ago why he remains important and relevant. His chapter was written in Portuguese and translated into English with support from the *Fundação Roberto Marinho* in Rio de Janeiro, for which we are deeply grateful.

Chapter 2, by Thereza Penna Firme and Vathsala Iyengar Stone, presents *Freirean Pedagogy in Street Education: Unveiling the Impact on Street Children in Brazil*. They present evaluation findings about a program working with homeless children that is based on Freire's pedagogy. Born in Rio de Janeiro, Dr. Penna Firme is an educator and psychologist specializing in evaluation both by academic training and professional practice. A graduate in clinical psychology (Pontific Catholic University of Rio de Janeiro—PUC-RIO), she obtained masters degrees in educational psychology (University of Wisconsin, 1965) and in education (Stanford University, 1966), as well as a Ph.D. in education and psychology of children and youth

(Stanford University, 1969). Dr. Penna Firme has taught extensively at primary, secondary, and higher-education levels in Brazil. She served as director of academic programs both at PUC-RIO and at the Federal University of Rio Grande do Sul and retired as the dean of the school of education at the Federal University of Rio de Janeiro. She taught graduate-level psychology and evaluation courses, conducted research, and directed graduate student dissertations at all these institutions. Her national and international contributions include her work as lecturer, consultant, and evaluator for organizations such as USAID, UNICEF, UNESCO El Salvador Ministry of Education, International Development Bank, World Bank, and Panamerican Health Organization. She has extensive experience evaluating programs for at-risk children. Currently Dr. Penna Firme coordinates the Evaluation Center at the CESGRANRIO Foundation and is evaluation consultant for the Roberto Marinho Foundation, both in Brazil.

The chapter's coauthor, Dr. Vathsala I. Stone, is Thereza's long-time close friend and colleague. Dr. Stone directs research and evaluation at the University at Buffalo's Center for Assistive Technology (CAT). She holds a Ph.D. in educational evaluation and research design from Florida State University (1974). Dr. Stone's career consists of 40 years as an evaluation professional in national and international contexts, 17 of those years spent in Brazil. She has taught and practiced evaluation, consulted, conducted research, and authored publications in evaluation and education. Besides her experience with formal education systems, a large part of her research and consultation for international organizations is centered on special needs populations—from children-at-risk (UNICEF), to children with limited or no access to education (Brazilian Space Research Institute), to economically disadvantaged populations (Roberto Marinho Foundation). Over the past 20 years at the Center for Assistive Technology, Dr. Stone has worked with multidisciplinary teams engaged in knowledge translation and technology transfer for persons with disabilities in need.

Part 2: Freirean Principles

Part 2 presents pedagogy of evaluation principles extracted from the writings of Paulo Freire and the chapters in Part 1. In Chapter 3, I identify, explain, and document the principles, an inspiration for *principles-focused evaluation* (Patton, 2017).

Chapter 4, "Pedagogy in Process Applied to Evaluation: Learning From Paulo Freire's Work in Guinea-Bissau," by Thomaz K. Chianca and Claudius Ceccon, examines and tests the principles based on Friere's work in Guiné Bissau. Thomaz Chianca is an international evaluation consultant with 20 years of experience in Brazil and in other 23 countries. His work encompasses several content areas including early childhood development and education, rural poverty reduction, decent work agenda, environmental protection, livestock care and management, children and adolescents' rights, and after-school initiatives, among others. He has a Ph.D. in inter-disciplinary evaluation from Western Michigan University (USA), a master of public health from the University of North Carolina at Chapel Hill (USA), and a dental surgeon degree from the Federal University of Rio de Janeiro (Brazil). He is a founding member of the Brazilian Monitoring and Evaluation Association and a member of its first managing board (2015–2017).

Claudius Ceccon is the Executive Director of the Center for the Creation of People's Image, a nongovernmental organization based in Rio de Janeiro that produces educational audio-visual and printed toolkits, conceives public interest campaigns, and organizes training courses and seminars for educators and social actors, empowering and qualifying their action as citizens in bringing about necessary changes to improve democracy in our society. Claudius graduated in Architecture by the National Faculty of Architecture and did postgraduate studies on Urban Planning and Industrial Design. He is also well known as a political cartoonist and illustrator. But it is Ceccon's direct work with Freire that is of particular relevance for this volume. They were political allies and exiled from Brazil at the same time, and worked directly together in Africa from 1975 to 1980 as part of a team helping the newly formed government in Guiné Bissau to plan and implement a national adult literacy program soon after the country achieved its independence from Portugal. That still doesn't explain how he appears in this volume. Claudius Ceccon is Thomaz Chianca's father-in-law.

Part 3: Examples of Freire's Current Evaluation Influence

Part 3 presents two examples of Freire's current influence.

Chapter 5, written by Vilma Guimarães, is entitled "Transformative Pedagogical Evaluation: Freirean Principles Practiced in Brazilian Public Schools." She is general manager of education and implementation at the Roberto Marinho Foundation in Rio de Janeiro, a nonprofit entity created in 1977 by journalist Roberto Marinho, which promotes national and cultural identity throughout Brazil and offers basic education through television. She was born in the state of Pernambuco, the birthland of educator Paulo Freire. She was close to Paulo Freire geographically, historically, and professionally in the early years of his eminent visibility. Their lives unfolded through immersion in the same political and cultural movement of the seventies. With him, she learned to listen, to value collective production, to live with differences, to conceptualize education as practice of autonomy and liberty, and to redesign schools with teachers, students, managers, technical staff, and the community based on Freirean the pedagogical principles. Talking with her, she is passionate about the ideal of constructing a society that is freer, more human, more just, and more egalitarian—and that evaluation is essential to realizing that vision. A graduate in history with specialization in educational macroplanning, she has vast experience in personnel and team management, as well as with production of educational programs.

NEW DIRECTIONS FOR EVALUATION • DOI: 10.1002/ev

She has served as a teacher, as a school principal, and as manager of the Educational Technology department of the Secretariat of the State of Pernambuco. In this last position, she conceptualized, implemented, and supported evaluation of innovative educational and community mobilization projects addressing adult literacy education, sexuality, environmental sustainability, drug addiction, and entrepreneurship. She brings the practitioner's perspective to the pedagogy of evaluation.

In Chapter 6, David Fetterman compares "Transformative Empowerment Evaluation and Freirean Pedagogy: Alignment with an Emancipatory Tradition." He is a past President of the American Evaluation Association (AEA) and author or editor of 16 evaluation books, including *Empowerment Evaluation: Knowledge and Tools for Self-Assessment*. He originated the empowerment evaluation approach, influenced by Freire. His article examines the parallels between Freire's pedagogy and empowerment evaluation, thereby illuminating both. Empowerment Evaluation celebrated its 21st anniversary at the 2015 American Evaluation Association meeting.

References

Fals-Borda, O., & Rahman, M. A. (Eds.). (1991). *Action and knowledge: Breaking the monopoly with participatory action research*. New York, NY: Apex Press.

Freire, P. (1970/2000). *Pedagogy of the oppressed (Bloomsbury paperback edition)*. New York, NY: Bloomsbury.

Freire, P. (2001). *Pedagogy of the freedom: Ethics, democracy, and civic courage*. Lantham, MD: Rowman & Littlefield.

Gadotti, M. (1994). *Reading Paulo Freire. His life and work*. Albany, NY: State University of New York Press.

House, E. R. (1990). Methodology and justice. *New Directions for Evaluation, 45*, 23–36.

House, E. R. (2014). *Evaluating: Values, biases, and practical wisdom*. Charlotte, NC: Information Age Publishing.

Kahn, R., & Kellner, D. (2007). Paulo Freire and Ivan Illich: Technology, politics and the reconstruction of education. *Policy Futures in Education, 5*(4), 431–448.

Kushner, S., & Rotondo, M. (2012). Editors' notes. *New Directions for Evaluation, 134*, 1–4.

Neirotti, N. (2012). Evaluation in Latin America: Paradigms and practices. *New Directions for Evaluation, 134*, 7–16.

Patton, M. Q. (2011). *Developmental evaluation: Applying complexity concepts to enhance innovation and use*. New York, NY: Guilford Press.

Patton, M. Q. (2012). *Essentials of utilization-focused evaluation*. Los Angeles, CA: Sage.

Patton, M. A. (2017). *Principles-focused evaluation: The guide*. New York, NY: Guilford Press.

Rosenstein, B., & Syna, H. D. (Eds.). (2015). Evaluation and social justice in complex sociopolitical contexts. *New Directions for Evaluation, 146*, 3–8.

Sirotnik, K. A. (Ed.). (1990). Evaluation and social justice: Issues in public education. *New Directions for Evaluation, 45*, 23–36.

Michael Quinn Patton

MICHAEL QUINN PATTON, founder and director of Utilization-Focused Evaluation, has over 45 years of experience as an independent evaluation consultant and is the author of several evaluation books, including Developmental Evaluation: Applying Complexity Concepts to Enhance Innovation and Use *and* Principles-Focused Evaluation: *The Guide.*

NEW DIRECTIONS FOR EVALUATION • DOI: 10.1002/ev

Gadotti, M. (2017). The global impact of Freire's pedagogy. In M. Q. Patton (Ed.), *Pedagogy of Evaluation. New Directions for Evaluation, 155*, 17–30.

1

The Global Impact of Freire's Pedagogy

Moacir Gadotti

Abstract

Freirean pedagogy continues to be an essential component in the construction of a fair, democratic global society. This chapter introduces Paulo Freire to those new to his thinking as well as update those who have long known of his work, about the global extent of its influence and impact, making clear that Freire's legacy goes well beyond his literacy method. Freire's theory is expressed in concepts and categories that reach a wider scope of education, including an anthropology-based theory of knowledge, which has direct implications for evaluation, especially evaluation's role in generating and disseminating knowledge. © 2017 Wiley Periodicals, Inc., and the American Evaluation Association.

Introduction: A Global Perspective on Freire's Pedagogical Impact

Although Paulo Freire came from a Latin American context, he was not limited by it. He dialogued with other perspectives and his pedagogy acquired universal meaning because the oppressed–oppressor relationship he addressed is universal and his theories were enriched by a variety of experiences and practices in different parts of the world. His thinking represents a synthesis of different sources, which poses to novice readers the problem of understanding it in a global sense (Gadotti, 1994). He influenced many thinkers and was also influenced by others. His humanist thinking drew inspiration from personalism, existentialism, phenomenology, and Marxism. He integrated key elements of these philosophical doctrines without repeating them in a mechanical or sectarian way. The association between humanism and Marxism that enriches his texts is one of the reasons he has been and still is read by a very large audience. But the pedagogy of dialogue that Freire practiced was not eclectic: it was based on a pluralist philosophy. Pluralism does not mean eclecticism or "sweetened" positions, as he used to say; it means to have a point of view and, based on it, to dialogue with others.

His theoretical work has been inspiring practices in various parts of the world, from the *mocambos* of Recife to the Burakumin communities of Japan,[1] to the most renowned educational institutions of Brazil and other countries. Such influence extends to several areas of knowledge: pedagogy, philosophy, theology, anthropology, social work, ecology, medicine, psychotherapy, psychology, museology, history, journalism, fine arts, theatre, music, physical education, sociology, participatory research, methods of teaching science and literature, philology, political science, school curriculum, and educational policy for street children. Also it resonates in evaluation, as shown in this publication's chapters, which I believe will stimulate fruitful debate on this subject.

Indications of the great vitality and widespread influence of his thinking include the growing number of publications of Paulo Freire's works in dozens of languages, the expansion of forums, academic departments, research centers created to study and debate the Freirean legacy, and the number of works written about him. All these elements together combine to lend a universal character to his pedagogical contributions.

I was close to Paulo Freire for 23 years and for me he was a true university. In this chapter, I will try to summarize some essential aspects of his theory and practices, starting with an overview of his legacy and then examining in more detail his contributions to the Popular Education Paradigm, with a focus on his work as Secretary of Education in São Paulo city. Following consideration of his pedagogy, I will invite your reflections on some lessons for educators and evaluators.

Legacy

Paulo Freire left us the legacy of ethical–political roots to support our practices; wings, that is, a theory to go beyond his work; and many dreams including the utopia of a society of equals; or, as he affirms at the end of *Pedagogy of the Oppressed*, "the creation of a world in which it will be easier to love."

There is no doubt that Paulo Freire made a major contribution to education and social justice (Torres, 2014) and to the dialectical conception of

---

[1] "*Mocambos*" are humble dwellings made of straw and clay in some poor rural Brazilian regions; also it can refer to inadequate dwellings in urban areas' shantytowns; the poor Bakunin people suffer discrimination in Japan.

NEW DIRECTIONS FOR EVALUATION • DOI: 10.1002/ev

education (Gadotti, 1996). Whether or not we accept his pedagogical ideas, their emancipatory and dialectical character represent a decisive milestone in the history of pedagogical thinking worldwide. Let me then highlight some enduring elements of his legacy before turning to an explication of his pedagogy and its implications for evaluation.

A political and educational philosophy—a method of investigation, research, and evaluation grounded in anthropology and in the theory of knowledge. Freire's thinking proved to be indispensable not only to the critical training of the educator, but also to the education of professionals from other fields, including evaluation. His educational philosophy crossed the boundaries between disciplines, sciences, and arts, beyond Latin America, taking root in various soils. He proposed new technical and methodological tools that established the qualitative founding principles of pedagogical and scientific research procedures in the area of education, intensifying the creation of new epistemologies and new political philosophies of education.

A pedagogy for the construction of a democratic society with social justice. Freire reflected, like few others, on the importance of educational policies, criticizing the "banking" approach to education (depositing "facts" into students' minds). His pedagogy remains valid—not only because we need even more democracy, more citizenship, and more social justice, but because schools and educational systems today face new challenges because of the generalization of information and the use of new technologies in society. To face these challenges, the school needs to become a living organism and an organizer of multiple training spaces; it needs to become a "circle of culture," as Freire used to say, much more a manager of social knowledge than an information provider. And for that, Paulo Freire has much to contribute, because throughout his work he insisted on interactive and deeply engaging methodologies, on mutually respectful ways of learning and teaching, on critical methods of teaching and research, on personal relationships, and on meaningful dialogue. For Freire, the radicalization of democracy was indispensable as a strategy to overcome social inequalities both in school and outside it. Paulo Freire pointed us to the education of the 21st century and not to the expansion of 19th-century education.

The utopia of an "universal human ethic" (Freire, 1997, p. 16) opposes the neoliberal thinking. Utopia is a central category in Paulo Freire's thinking. For this reason, he is diametrically opposed to neoliberal education, because neoliberalism rejects dreams and utopia. What is sought is standardization (Fordism, Toyotism) of quality, evaluation, and learning. In this conception, teachers do not have scientific knowledge; their knowledge is useless. Therefore, they do not need to be consulted. They only need to know recipes, "how to do," without asking themselves why. The public sphere is losing the hegemony of the educational project to the private sphere, transposing into education the ethics of the market. Paulo Freire, instead, speaks of an "universal human ethic" (Freire, 1997, p. 16), which opposes the neoliberal thinking. Neoliberal thinking abhors dreams and utopia, whereas Freirean thinking is utopian: *the critical attitude [is] permanently present in me toward the wickedness of neoliberalism, its cynical fatalistic ideology and its inflexible refusal of dream and utopia* (Freire, 1997, p. 15).

Contributions to the paradigm of popular education. Education is not a neutral process. Popular education, like all education, presupposes a societal project. What characterizes it is its clear and explicit political choice. It is a rich and varied tradition recognized for its emancipatory, alternative, alterative, and participatory characteristics (Brandão, 1982). In its origins are the anarchism of industrial proletariat of the beginning of the last century; self-managed socialism; European radical liberalism; popular movements; utopias of independence; theories of liberation, and dialectical pedagogy. The paradigm of popular education has marked Latin America and supports many experiences and projects inspired by revolutionary educators like José Martí, Simon Bolívar, Simon Rodriguez, Orlando Fals Borda, and Paulo Freire. In contrast with old left-wing theses that did not cherish democracy, Freire's thinking was pioneering in Latin America, when he proposed that revolution cannot be reached without an ethic that pursues the radicalization of democracy.

Illuminating lessons for both teachers and evaluators as managers of knowledge. Given that critical pedagogy is fundamentally evaluative, Freire's lessons for teachers may also be potential lessons for evaluators, as we will see below.

Making Education "Popular"

Today, popular education is reinventing itself. Its process was enriched with new proposals for citizenship and human rights education. Always remaining true to the reading of the world's new circumstances, it incorporates the achievements of new technologies, resuming old themes, and including others: migration, diversity, playfulness, sustainability, and interdisciplinarity; and issues of gender, ethnicity, age, local development, employment, and income. But the core principles articulated and defended by Freire (see Table 1.1) remain relevant, constantly reinvented by new social and educational practices.

Paulo Freire was a man of praxis, both a thinker and a doer. It can be said he was the Brazilian educator who opened more doors for popular education as a public policy, when, in 1989, he accepted becoming the Secretary of Education of São Paulo, the biggest South American city.

Popular education as a public policy: Freire in São Paulo city's Education Department

In the last decades of his life, Paulo Freire went through a period of recasting of popular education. In August 1985, in an interview with Rosa Maria

Table 1.1. Freirean Popular Education Principles and Premises

Principles	Premises in support of the principles
1. Utopia is the true realism of the educator.	Rejection of fatalist (neoliberal) thinking. "The world is not finished. It is always in the process of becoming."
2. Harmony between formal and nonformal education.	The school is not the only educational space.
3. Acknowledgment of the legitimacy of popular knowledge, at a time of extreme elitism	We learn as we struggle.
4. Theorizing practice in order to transform it.	Educational practice is inherently political: All education presupposes a societal project.
5. A method of teaching and research based on the reading of reality.	This pedagogy is committed to active citizenship: Popular education fosters the political and civic participation of the popular classes to overcome oppressive social conditions.
6. Education as a practice of freedom, the precondition for democratic life.	Ethics as a central reference in the pursuit of the radicalization of democracy.

Torres,[2] he maintains that "popular education seeks to mobilize and organize people, with the goal of creating people's power" (Torres, 1987, p. 74). In this same interview, Freire affirms that in order to implement popular education it is not necessary to work with adults, and that popular education is a concept of education independent of the age of the students: it "cannot be mistaken for adult education, and is not restricted solely to adults. I would say that the brand, or what defines popular education, is not the age of the students, but the political option, that is to say, the political practice understood and assumed in educational practice" (Freire, in Torres, 1987, pp. 86–87).

In the late 1980s and early 1990s, public school got onto the agenda of popular education. The State was no longer seen as an enemy, as it was during the Latin American dictatorships. Some NGOs have become partners with popular and democratic administrations. State, as Society, came to be seen as not monolithic, but in a constant process of transformation. In this context, Paulo Freire defended the thesis that popular education could and should inspire public policies in education (Beisiegel, 2008). He wanted not only to democratize education, but to ensure that it could "be popular," that is, to include in its practices the emancipatory principles of popular education as part of a societal project. And, through his work as Municipal Secretary of Education of São Paulo (Freire, 1991), he demonstrated

[2] Rosa Maria Torres, formerly Ecuador's Minister of Education (2003), is a linguist and communicator (see www.otraeducacion.blogspot.com).

NEW DIRECTIONS FOR EVALUATION • DOI: 10.1002/ev

that popular education is a process that is built simultaneously inside and outside the State.

Collective Work as a Pedagogical Principle

When I worked with Paulo Freire at the Municipal Department of Education of São Paulo, where I was chief of staff, he impressed all of us with his political–pedagogical and ideological clarity. His educational policy was guided by the Popular Education principles (Table 1.1) we learned to include in practice. They represent, in short, the defense of popular public education, which meets, with quality, the interests of the majority of the population, overcoming elitist standards.

What I would like to emphasize now is his political–pedagogical project: *collective work as a pedagogical principle*. For Paulo Freire, education is a social practice that takes place in spaces beyond the school, and as it is a social practice present in different spaces, we need more and more of a collective construction.

The principle of collective work is a way to focus on *curriculum* and on *management* simultaneously. Therefore, the principle is translated, on the one hand, through Freire's interdisciplinary vision of the curriculum, of sciences, of culture, and education, and, on the other, through his uncompromising defense of democratic management.

Collective work and curriculum reorientation: interdisciplinarity and transdisciplinarity. In Paulo Freire's curriculum reorientation, the reflective inquiry process involved three articulated phases or moments: study of reality, organization of knowledge, and application of knowledge. The study of reality is guided by *problematization* based on the life history of educators, learners, and communities, involving visits, interviews, questionnaires, and meaningful situations in order to reach the generative themes. Organization of knowledge is carried out by selecting and articulating areas of the curriculum, systematization of already built knowledge, and by raising hypotheses, assumptions, concepts, and theories. Application of knowledge involves the planning and implementation of the program, reconstruction of already built knowledge, using not only books and teaching materials for tools but also reading the world as it is experienced, aiming at transformation of the educator and the student in the process, and reflecting together on what unfolds, that is to say, *evaluating*.

In Paulo Freire's view, the application of knowledge necessarily presupposes the demonstration of deeper understanding by the student but also the presentation of proposals for change and commitment to them. It had to do with the deepening of understanding, knowledge, and the student's ability to use already built knowledge to transform reality. If application of knowledge presupposes the demonstration of understanding, this comprehension requires that knowledge be interdisciplinary and transdisciplinary

In the wide process of curricular reorientation Paulo Freire launched in 1989 as Municipal Secretary of São Paulo, he proposed a discussion of

NEW DIRECTIONS FOR EVALUATION • DOI: 10.1002/ev

"interdisciplinarity via generative themes" which was named "Projeto Inter" (O'Cadiz, Torres, & Wong, 1998). Between the years 1987 and 1988, Freire participated in a reflection group formed by teachers of several fields of the Universidade de Campinas (UNICAMP), who discussed how to carry out interdisciplinarity not only in schools, public or private, but also in their work with low-income communities. The primary goal of interdisciplinarity is to experience a global reality that is part of the daily lives of students, teachers, and people, which in the traditional school is compartmentalized and fragmented. To articulate knowledge, experience, school, community, and the environment is the goal of interdisciplinarity, which is translated in practice by collective and solitary work.

Transdisciplinarity involves a dialogue that merges with the interdisciplinary educational process itself. In an emancipatory perspective, it is not possible to teach and to learn without dialogue, without dialogic communication. In this process, educators, subjects of their own educational practices, are able to develop programs and methods of teaching–learning, being competent to bring their school into a community.

There is no interdisciplinarity and transdisciplinarity without decentralization of power. Consequently, there is no interdisciplinarity and transdisciplinarity without democratic management and without the effective autonomy of the school or learning community.

Collective work and democratic management. Pedagogical action through interdisciplinarity and transdisciplinarity calls for building participatory and decisive schools/learning communities for the social inquiry. That's why an administrative reform was needed in São Paulo's Department of Education (which worked in an hierarchical logic), so it could be able to incorporate an emancipatory democratic educational project. Said Freire: "When I was Secretary of Education for the city of São Paulo, obviously committed to leading an administration that, in line with our political dream, with our utopia, took seriously, as it should be, the issue of popular participation in the future of the school, my teammates and I had to start from the very beginning. I mean, I began by making an administrative reform so the Department of Education would work differently" (Freire, 1993, p. 74).

Democratic management as defended by Paulo Freire is fundamental. Without it, the construction of knowledge from the perspective of emancipation does not occur. It can be said that participation and autonomy constitute the very nature of the educational practice. Participation is a precondition for learning; it directly influences learning.

Teaching, According to Paulo Freire, and Implications for Evaluation

Education of teachers was one of Paulo Freire's constant concerns, manifested in his numerous works. He also reaffirmed the necessary professionalization of teaching against the devaluation of this profession (see Freire, 1992). The title in English is *Teachers as Cultural Workers Letters to Those Who Dare to Teach*. In a dialogue with American educator Ira Shor, registered in *Fear and Daring: The Daily Life of the Teacher* (Freire & Shor, 1987), Freire analyzed the dialectic between utopia and everyday life, between dream and reality embedded in teaching/learning. In this book, the authors affirm that education for liberation is a stimulus for people to mobilize, organize, and "empower" themselves. To learn is to dare and to overcome fear.

Lessons for Evaluators

What lessons did Paulo Freire leave us as educators and, by inference, as evaluators?

The lessons identified thus far can be applied to both education and evaluation for, as this volume asserts throughout, both are inherently pedagogical practices. This means that all aspects of education and evaluation carry messages and teach, whether explicitly or implicitly, whether in process or content, in style or substance, in relationship or in format, in imposition or in collaboration. These lessons are far from exhaustive of what Paulo Freire's pedagogy offers, but should be considered illustrative and generative.

1. **Reason and emotion are interconnected.** Freire used to talk about an ethic inseparable from aesthetic, especially in his last book (Freire, 1997). In teaching, being and knowing are inextricably linked. Our classical tradition of education avoids connecting our emotions with our reason. Paulo Freire, in contrast, spoke of a "reason soaked with emotion." He was very insistent on this point. Education accounts for the creation of the freedom of every self-aware, perceptive, and responsible being, in which reason and emotion are in constant equilibrium and interaction. In the world of life, the symbolic knowledge and the perceptive knowledge constantly interact. Knowledge is produced by human beings, beings of rationality and affection. Neither of these characteristics is superior to the other. It is always the subject who constructs categories of thought through her or his experiences with another person, in a given context, at a given moment. The affective aspect, in this construction, always remains. Omnipotent reason generates a bureaucratic and rationalist school, unable to understand the world of life and the human being in its entirety. It is a dogmatic and dormant school and not a living organism. We must understand the cognitive processes as vital processes insofar as the intellect and sensitivity are inseparable. Knowledge is a social construction and not mere "acquisition" or "assimilation" of something pre-existent in the individual who knows something. Before knowing, the individual "is interested in," "is curious about" ... which Freire called "epistemological curiosity" (1997, p. 165). It is this curiosity that drives the individual to appropriate what mankind has historically produced.

2. **Knowledge is emancipatory.** In this conception, knowledge has an emancipatory function: knowing how to think independently, being a creator, a subject with autonomy, learning in order to govern oneself and to be sovereign. The word "emancipate" comes from ex-manus or from ex-mancipum. Ex (indicates the idea of "exit" or "withdrawal") and manus ("hand," symbolizing power). To emancipate then is "to take away the hand that grasps," "to free, to give up powers"; it means "to put out of custody." Ex-manus (out-hand) means "to put beyond the reach of the hand." To emancipate oneself is, then, to say to those who oppress us: "take your hand off me!"

3. **There is no teaching without learning, and no learning without teaching.** For Paulo Freire, more important than knowing how to teach is knowing how the student learns. Paulo Freire created a method of knowledge and not exactly a method of teaching. For this reason, already in his early writings, he created the neologism "dodiscência" (1997, p. 31), "teach-learn"ing, to name the dialogic relationship between the act of teaching and the act of learning—"there is no teaching without learning" (1997, p. 23); "whoever teaches learns in the act of teaching, and whoever learns teaches in the act of learning" (1997, p. 25)—one is not the object of the other. This is why he replaced "lessons" with "culture circles."

4. **Pedagogy involves both being and knowing.** What does the teacher need to know in order to teach? Many things. However, the more important question is: *What should we be like in order to teach?* Students will only learn when they desire to learn, when they feel pleasure in what they are learning. Students want to know, but they do not always want to learn what is being taught. Students need to be authors, rebels, and creators. And for this, the apprentices, who also teach, have to be respected for their cultural experiences and own pace of learning.

5. **Meaningful pedagogy is meaningful to daily living.** What does it mean to educate in Freire's emancipatory perspective? To educate and to educate oneself is always to impregnate what we do in our daily lives with meaning. It is to understand and to transform the world and oneself. It is to share the world: to share more than knowledge and ideas, but to share the heart. In a violent society such as ours, we need to educate for understanding, for tenderness, for compassion and solidarity. To educate is also to destabilize, to doubt, to suspect, to struggle, to take sides, to be present in the world. To educate is to take a position, not to be passive. To educate is to transform. It is not to subserviently repeat what was done in the past, to choose the safety of conformity, through loyalty to tradition; or, conversely, to face the established order and run the risk of adventure; nor to want the past to configure the entire future or rely on the past to construct something new. Such approaches are abstractions. The transformational power of education is realized by being grounded in what transformation means for daily living.

NEW DIRECTIONS FOR EVALUATION • DOI: 10.1002/ev

6.   Interdisciplinarity is essential because it is true to the nature of the world. Paulo Freire understood interdisciplinarity, the connection between disciplines and areas of knowledge, as a precondition for creating meaning and one step to reach transdisciplinarity in the pursuit of wholeness. It is an attitude and a method, indispensable to the researcher and to the educator. It is also an essential dimension of all that exists. Interdisciplinarity must be in the practice of teaching and research because it is out there, in the complex fabric of reality.

7.   Transdisciplinarity seeks to understand holistically, to synthesize and share, not divide. Transdisciplinarity seeks to understand, more than to accumulate knowledge; it includes, aggregates, shares, and does not divide. Thus, Paulo Freire joined the interdisciplinary attitude with the transdisciplinary attitude, because he found in both the essence of collective work, conviviality, transversality, and dialogue. And it is not possible to teach and to learn without dialogue, without dialogic communication.

8.   Educational inequalities produce social inequalities. It is true that social inequalities produce educational inequalities. Also true is that educational inequalities produced by a technocratic education will cause social inequalities, as those who fail or abandon school will be socially and economically hindered. To eliminate educational inequity, the principle of democratic management is essential. It is not limited to basic education: it refers to all levels and types of education. Democratic management should be coherent with a democratic and emancipatory notion of education: it should not be understood only as a participatory practice, but as a radicalization of democracy, as a strategy to overcome authoritarianism, patrimonialism, individualism, and social inequalities.

Education and Evaluation: Issues of Purpose and Quality Interconnected

We care about quality of education—and we should care—but first we need to know what kind of quality we are talking about and what kind of education. The discussion of quality of education and evaluation requires a discussion of the purposes of education and of the purposes of evaluation.

Evaluation has been one of the most debated issues in contemporary education. Never before were the means of evaluation so improved. We got very close to perfection. But we did not come to discuss in the same depth what we are evaluating, why we are evaluating, "for whom," "against whom," as Freire would say. In order to understand the meaning of evaluation, we need to look into the meaning of education and learning.

Education, in the neoliberal ideology, is considered a service, a commodity, and not a right. Its reference is the market, not citizenship. Its projects are much more oriented toward purchasing equipment and teaching materials. Those are not educational projects in the strict sense. This ideology does not question itself about the purpose of education, a question that has been omitted intentionally, since its societal project is not inclusive and fair, but presupposes the domination of a few over the 99%. It is the dominance of means over ends. As stated earlier, in this context, teacher and student (or project leader and individuals being led) are not producers of knowledge, but deliverers and consumers of ready-made information. Traditionally, evaluation is something done *to* those who are learning, not *with* them.

This conception of education and evaluation does not respond to the needs of a society of networks and movements, a society of multiple opportunities for learning, in which it is essential to learn and to think independently, to know how to communicate, how to research, how to do things, to be capable of logical thinking, to learn how to work collaboratively, to make theoretical syntheses and elaborations, to know how to organize one's own work, to have self-discipline, to be a subject in the construction of knowledge, to be open to new knowledge, to know the sources of information, in short, to know how to articulate scientific knowledge with the practice of different kinds of knowledge.

Freirean education is aligned with this other society project in which there is no place for oppressors and oppressed, but for citizens with equal rights living together in a radical form of democracy. Teacher and student, project leader and members of the team, evaluators and people being evaluated are producers and managers of a knowledge that will be used to transform reality. The Principles and Premises of Popular Education (Table 1.1) are also the foundations of collaborative dialogical evaluation—an evaluation done with those who are learning, not to them, based on collective work and democratic management as inspired by Freirean pedagogical principles. Because both education and evaluation involve reflective inquiry, its three articulated phases or moments proposed by Freire (study of reality, organization of knowledge, and application of knowledge) can be applied to the conduct of evaluations, that, likewise, should be interdisciplinary and transdisciplinary in both theory and practice.

Theory and Method

One of the most important features of Paulo Freire's work is its coherence between theory and method, theory and practice, and content and form. They are inseparable, like the acts of learning and teaching are inseparable. This coherence is also established because his theory of knowledge is based, as we have seen, on anthropology. It is from this close link that arises the main categories and concepts that articulate his thinking, such as oppressed, praxis, curiosity, dialogue, utopia, autonomy, *politicality*, criticality, connectivity, awareness ("conscientização"), emancipation, untested feasibility (*"inédito viável"*), circle of culture, *teach learning* ("dodicência), and futurity, to name but a few.

NEW DIRECTIONS FOR EVALUATION • DOI: 10.1002/ev

For Paulo Freire, the question of method is crucial in the educational act, as it is in the evaluative act: when we use a certain method, which is not neutral, we do it based on an ethical, political, and pedagogical choice. In this sense, the chosen method itself already carries in its history a theory that underlies it, and certain principles and values. In a "traditional" notion of education and curriculum, the principal teaching method is the transmission of knowledge by the teacher, to the students, already criticized by Paulo Freire since the 1960s as "banking" education.

Etymologically, "method" means the "way" the teacher will follow to achieve a particular purpose that in traditional education aims to keep students as mere apprentices, teachers as instructors, the school as the institution of transmission of historically accumulated knowledge and evaluation as a strategy of control. Pointing in another direction are the emancipatory pedagogies, like the pedagogy of the oppressed, or of hope, created by Paulo Freire, proposing participatory and democratic methods in which students and teachers are the center of the teaching-learning process and evaluation is a form of developing autonomy and critical thinking. Resulting from this concept of education, we have, for example, the method of "participatory research" and "participatory evaluation" in which all those involved in the process learn, research, and evaluate together, teaching and learning as they do so, because, unlike traditional methods of education and evaluation, they consider people owners of their own learning process.

Both in his speeches and in his writings, Paulo Freire was very rigorous in his explanations, in the way with which he arranged his concepts and categories while speaking and writing. His analysis and expression were rigorously scientific, in the footsteps of one of his masters, Álvaro Vieira Pinto (1969). When well structured, a theory is expressed in concepts and categories that somehow underpin an entire text or speech, and in Paulo Freire's case, an entire oeuvre. To discover these concepts and categorize them gives us a more general idea of how they are organized in an organic whole. It is very important to work with concepts when we want to really understand an author's thinking. This is why I dare to conclude this chapter with a synoptic table, in which I establish a comparison of Freire's anthropology, with his theory of knowledge, his pedagogy, and his method (Table 1.2). It is an invitation for the reader to replace the word "educate" with "evaluate" throughout Table 1.2 and reflect on the implications of Freirean pedagogy for evaluation.

Looking to the Future of Educating to Transform 21th-Century Popular Education: The Ongoing Work of the Paulo Freire Institute

When Paulo Freire left the Sao Paulo's Municipal Department of Education, in 1991, he was freer to devote himself to a new challenge: the creation of

Table 1.2. Comparison of Freire's Anthropology, Theory of Knowledge, Pedagogy, and Method

Anthropology	Theory of knowledge	Pedagogy	Method
1. Being human: being-in-the-world, of the world, a curious being, programmed to learn.	Reading the world (the study of reality): everyone can learn and teach (legitimacy of popular knowledge), curiosity.	Pedagogy is a guide for the construction of a dream; reading the world precludes the reading of words: utopia and daily life.	Thematic inquiry: reality as the departure point; theorize practice; vocabulary universe: generative words and themes.

an Institute to bring together people and institutions which, driven by the same dreams of a humanizing education, could deepen their reflections, improve their practices and strengthen themselves in the struggle for the construction of another possible world.

The Instituto Paulo Freire (IPF) was founded amid the political unrest that followed the events leading to the fall of the Berlin Wall and the end of the Soviet empire. That was a defining moment for leftists worldwide. In a way, it was as if we had lost ground, lost our paradigm. Paulo Freire was asked at that time if he thought that it was the "end of socialism." He replied that it was not the end of socialism but the end of a certain face of socialism. And added that, in this way, it would be easier to defend democratic socialism, socialism with freedom. In the middle of a global paradigmatic crisis, the newly formed *Instituto Paulo Freire* reasserted and strengthened the notion that the paradigm of the oppressed has nothing to do with the socialist authoritarian paradigm. Freire would follow the Institute's activities closely, despite his always-busy schedule. From 1991 until his untimely death in 1997, he supervised all projects of the IPF.

To continue Freire's work does not mean to repeat it, but to reinvent it. As he once said, "the only way anyone has of applying in their situation any of the propositions I have made is precisely by redoing what I have done, that is, by not following me. In order to follow me it is essential not to follow me!" (Freire & Faundez, 1985, p. 41). This is IPF's aspiration. The utopia that moves this institution is to educate to transform, to create a planetary citizenship, a "planetarization" (Antunes, 2002), fighting social injustice caused by capitalist globalization, in the light of a new political culture, inspired by the Freirean legacy. We invite evaluators to join us, and assist us, to build more just and sustainable realities (more about us in www.paulofreire.org).

NEW DIRECTIONS FOR EVALUATION • DOI: 10.1002/ev

References

Antunes, A. (2002). *Leitura do mundo no contexto da planetarização: Por uma pedagogia da sustentabilidade (Unpublished doctoral dissertation)*. FE-USP, São Paulo, Brazil.

Beisiegel, C. R. (2008). *Política e Educação Popular: A teoria e a prática de Paulo Freire no Brasil*. Brasília: Liber.

Brandão, C. R. (1982). *O que é Educação Popular*. São Paulo, Brazil: Brasiliense.

Freire, P. (1991). *Educação na cidade*. São Paulo, Brazil: Cortez.

Freire, P. (1992). *Professora sim, tia não: Cartas a quem ousa ensinar*. São Paulo, Brazil: Olho D'Água.

Freire, P. (1993). *Política e educação*. São Paulo, Brazil: Cortez.

Freire, P. (1997). *Pedagogia da Autonomia: Saberes necessários à prática educativa*. São Paulo, Brazil: Paz e Terra.

Freire, P. (2000). *Pedagogia da indignação: Cartas pedagógicas e outros escritos*. São Paulo, Brazil: Unesp.

Freire, P., & Faundez, A. (1985). *Por uma pedagogia da pergunta*. São Paulo, Brazil: Paz e Terra.

Freire, P., & Shor, I. (1987). *Medo e ousadia: O cotidiano do professor*. São Paulo, Brazil: Paz e Terra.

Gadotti, M. (1994). *Reading Paulo Freire: His life and work*. Albany, NY: SUNY Press.

Gadotti, M. (Ed.). (1996). *Paulo Freire: Uma biobibliografia*. São Paulo, Brazil: Cortez/Instituto Paulo Freire.

Gadotti, M. (1996). *Pedagogy of praxis: A dialectical philosophy of education*. Albany, NY: SUNY Press.

Gadotti, M. (2007). *Educar para um outro mundo possível: O Fórum Social Mundial como espaço de aprendizagem de uma nova cultura política e como processo transformador da sociedade civil planetária*. São Paulo, Brazil: Publisher Brasil.Gadotti, M. (2009). *Education for sustainability: A contribution to the Decade of Education for Sustainable Development*. São Paulo, Brazil: Instituto Paulo Freire.

Gutiérrez, F., & Prado, C. (1989). *Ecopedagogia e cidadania planetária*. São Paulo, Brazil: Instituto Paulo Freire/Cortez.

O'Cadiz, M.D.P., Torres, C. A., & Lindquist Wong, P. (1998). *Education and democracy: Paulo Freire, social movements and educational reform in São Paulo*. Boulder, CO: Westview Press.

Padilha, P. R. (2004). *Currículo intertranscultural: Novos itinerários para a educação*. São Paulo, Brazil: Instituto Paulo Freire/Cortez.

Pini, F. R. O., & Moraes, C. V. (Eds.). (2011). *Educação, participação política e Direitos Humanos*. São Paulo, Brazil: Instituto Paulo Freire.

Pinto, A. V. (1969). *Ciência e existência: Problemas filosóficos da pesquisa científica*. Rio de Janeiro, Brazil: Paz e Terra.

Romão, J. E. (2000). *Dialética da diferença: O projeto da Escola Cidadã frente ao projeto pedagógico neoliberal*. São Paulo, Brazil: Cortez.

Torres, C. A. (2014). *First Freire: Early writings in social justice education*. New York, NY: Teachers College Press.

Torres, C. A., & Noguera, P. (Eds.). (2008). *Social justice education for teachers: Paulo Freire and the possible dream*. Rotterdam, The Netherlands: Sense Publishers.

Torres, R. M. (Ed.). (1987). *Educação Popular: Um encontro com Paulo Freire*. São Paulo, Brazil: Loyola.

MOACIR GADOTTI, *one of Paulo Freire's closest collaborators after Freire's return to Brazil from exile, worked with him for almost 20 years, and is a professor of education at the University of São Paulo and director of the Instituto Paulo Freire in São Paulo.*

Firme, T. P., Stone, V. I. (2017). Freirean *Pedagogy* in street education: Unveiling the impact on street children in Brazil. In M. Q. Patton (Ed.), *Pedagogy of Evaluation. New Directions for Evaluation, 155*, 31–47.

2

Freirean *Pedagogy* in Street Education: Unveiling the Impact on Street Children in Brazil

Thereza Penna Firme, Vathsala Iyengar Stone

Abstract

This chapter reports an evaluation of programs serving street children in Brazil during the mid-1980s. At the time, several hundred independent programs for street children had emerged all over Brazil. Paulo Freire's views and concern for an appropriate educational process that regards the cultural identity of these children and youth as well as their self-acceptance were fundamental to the conception and development of many of these programs. UNICEF commissioned a groundbreaking study that would provide a methodological basis for more comprehensive evaluations in the future. This chapter shows how Freirean pedagogy influenced both the interventions and the evaluation. © 2017 Wiley Periodicals, Inc., and the American Evaluation Association.

Introduction

This chapter illustrates a feasible and effective way of conducting authentic and credible evaluation of innovative care alternatives for street children in Brazil based on Freirean pedagogy. Freire (2000,

Information updates about multiplication of street children programs in Brazil were provided by Cesare de Florio La Rocca, former UNICEF official, currently director for 25 years of Project AXÉ for children in especially difficult circumstances, Salvador, Bahia, Brazil. Information about current structure of street children programs was provided by Alfredo Gomes da Costa—educator and consultant for social-educational programs in Brazil.

New Directions for Evaluation, no. 155, Fall 2017 © 2017 Wiley Periodicals, Inc., and the American Evaluation Association. Published online in Wiley Online Library (wileyonlinelibrary.com) • DOI: 10.1002/ev.20252

31

2005, 2013) inspired the social work of the *street educators* in these service alternative programs (Swift, 1991). The evaluation strategy that unveiled the impact of these programs on the street children and youth shared a common ground with the program's context: the ethical principles of human interaction rooted in the emancipating ideas of Paulo Freire.

The focus of this chapter is not social violence in Brazil that the sad faces of its street children reveal, nor the injuries they are known to suffer from abuse, murder, drug addiction, and other forms of cruelty; it is the efforts that have attempted to lead these children from crisis to hope (Swift, 1990; UNICEF/MPAS, n.d.). At the time of this study, some several hundred independent programs for street children had emerged all over Brazil. Paulo Freire's views and concern for an appropriate educational process that regards the cultural identity of these children and youth as well as their self-acceptance (Freire, 2000) were fundamental to the conception and development of many of these courageous, and sometimes risky, socio-educational experiences. Despite good intentions on the part of these programs, evaluation to detect their beneficial impact had been overlooked until UNICEF commissioned the authors to undertake the task. The initial study provided a methodological basis for more comprehensive evaluations in the future.

The Setting

The study was conducted in 1986–1987 (Penna-Firme, Tijiboy, & Stone, 1987, 1991). Brazil was facing great economic instability following rapid industrialization, and the government had just transitioned from a military regime to democracy. With 41% of families living below the poverty line, over 16 million children were growing up in impoverishment, mostly concentrated in *favelas* or slum communities rapidly being created around urban cities by rural immigrants. A crisis of unprotected children and adolescents had developed within this process (Swift, 1990). Scenes of the helpless, oppressed child desperately cried for help.

Scene 1

Despite the threat of rain, intense cold, and the late hour, almost night-time, children ages 7 to 17 were gathered near a fountain in the square of the bustling and noisy city center. Eduardo Henrique and his 14-year-old pregnant mother were there. He had known the square from the very beginning of his life... The children discussed many things, apparently superficial, but in truth very serious: where were they going to sleep today? What were they going to eat? How to get the pregnant girl's boyfriend—who was arrested yesterday—released from jail in time for the baby's birth? Where was the baby going to be born? ... Who was the new policeman for that area? Help was needed for a woman who just appeared at the square in search of her daughter who had run away from home. Anyone know where she is? …what about a work card? …the conversations seem never-ending …cold and hunger were masked by "sniffing glue." This scene is continually repeated, interposed, however, with new events such as a passer-by inviting a 13-year-old girl to work in explicit sex scenes.

Scene 2

On the streets of the big city, children from poor communities play and run free, crossing byways and squares, without school, trying to survive while exposed to the dangers of the streets. At night these young people return home cold and hungry, but there is someone waiting there, even if they are only waiting to collect their contribution toward supporting the family.

The challenge

An estimated seven million children and adolescents spent the major part of their lives on the street working long hours to support their poor parents or fend for themselves. They were either "children of the street" (Scene 1 above), where they actually slept, having run away from broken or impoverished families to escape abuse, abandonment, and neglect; or "children on the street" (Scene 2 above) spending long hours working there to help their impoverished families (Espert & Myers, 1988). Both kinds of children were exposed to perils of the street, frequently hounded by police, and exploited by abusive and criminal adults, notably for the drug and sex trades. As Myers (1988) described in his preface to the authors' evaluation report, the children "inhabited an environment of extreme social marginalization in which their physical, emotional, intellectual development were seriously compromised" (Penna-Firme et al., 1987).

The period was also one of paradigm shift and hope. In the long term, recovering these children goes far beyond them—to the families, public authorities, and society overall—and attention to the needs of street children is not only a question of economic development but also very much a question of political will. However, the early attempts by the government to institutionalize the street child viewed the child as a socially and culturally deprived person. This approach increasingly failed and eventually gave rise to a democratic approach where the child was no longer considered a deprived individual but the subject of his own history. Many concerned individuals and community groups, including the State, the Church and NGOs, responded with alternative service approaches. Their promise did in fact sow the seeds of social change (Swift, 1990). An overall critical structural approach, in tune with Freire's ideas and concerns, emerged to overcome the perverse cycle of institutionalization, deportation, and imprisonment, and to promote and defend the human rights and citizenship of the children (UNICEF/MPAS, n.d.). In 1982, UNICEF and the Brazilian government formed the Project "Alternative Service Programs for Street Children" to promote shared learning from community experience and use

NEW DIRECTIONS FOR EVALUATION • DOI: 10.1002/ev

collective knowledge to work more effectively with street children. The project in effect played a catalytic role in a popular movement growing at the time. Discussion about unprotected children led to stronger mobilization to work with them, and to emergence of leaders securely linked to grass-roots communities (Swift, 1990).

The new project needed systematic and objective data for ongoing monitoring of its outcomes. The alternative programs were too busily consumed by street children needs emerging in multiple areas to devote the time for organized, formal recording of their intents or actions. An urgent concern for UNICEF was to learn to what extent the programs delivered the promise they were reputed for—in other words, how exactly are the programs benefiting the children they serve? What is their impact? What is happening to the children at the end of the line? The task of the study described here was to explore and respond to this concern. A team of three evaluators, which includes the two authors of this chapter and their late colleague Juan Antonio Tijiboy, conducted the study.

The Alternative Programs for Street Children

What were the alternative street children programs like? How were they different from the failing government programs? The essence of the alternative programs lay in the actions of the *street educator*, a concept through which the programs operationalized Freirean pedagogy. Besides academic training, the street educator needed to learn a way to approach, understand, respect, and help the street child as a participating and active subject—and never as the object—of a process that would guarantee the child a future as an integrated member of society.

Borrowing Freire's eyes to look at these children meant being sensitive to their severe conditions of life and going beyond, to discover their personality unfairly distorted by adults around them and, paradoxically, by those designated to protect them. Here is precisely where Paulo Freire inspired the programs for a transformative educational process leading to change. The street educator acted on the side of the oppressed with authenticity, truthfulness, and coherence, respecting the children as individuals with their own values and expectations. It indeed took an extremely patient approach not to invade their much-deserved privacy. It meant listening to the children or youngsters, capturing their feelings, gestures, emotions, and concerns. It also meant, as Freire alerted, that the educator should not lose his individuality or authority, but together with the child, should try to find a response about his or her "being-in-the-world" (UNICEF, 1987). Decisions would then emerge from this encounter. Dialogue and critical thinking were a big part of it, with emphasis placed on knowledge construction through pondering over reality, or "reading of the world," as Freire would put it. As one street educator put it, unlike the government program where the educator considered himself the owner of knowledge, the street educator exchanged knowledge with the children (Swift, 1990). In sum, it implied an ability of the programs to work within the Freirean concept of *utopia* (Freire, 1992, 2014) in order to inspire and move the child from despair to hope. As reported by Swift, the street children programs had a democratic management style, responded to lower costs, and were able to mobilize local communities for changes beyond assistance to the immediate street children needs.

Although the programs shared a broad concern for the plight of the children, they greatly differed in their philosophies, objectives, and activities. The day-to-day actions of street educators consisted of pursuing emergent, rather than predefined, needs of the children. Services varied from offering food/shelter/first aid to giving attention/care/counseling, to skill building to help them earn their livelihood. No one program could offer all services to the same extent, and their methods were dictated by the children they served. Typically, they all initiated contact with a needy child using a wide range of creative approaches, to gain the child's trust. This period of "courtship" was necessarily longer for programs serving the children "of the street" than for those serving children "on the street." This effort would enable them to attract the child and involve him or her in program activities; initially these would be meals, income-generating opportunities, talking about his or her life and problems, or attending to injuries and health issues. Following the child's interest and potential, and using available resources, many programs went on to involve the child in cooperatives, crafts work and sales, courses and apprenticeships. Each program was therefore unique. Collectively, the programs were multidimensional in intent and methods. And their educational methods always preserved the liberty of the children, leaving them free to make all their own decisions. Dialogue and critical thinking marked the methods.

Evaluation Methodology

Early discussions with UNICEF and project officials made the challenges to the study design very clear. Lack of information about the objectives that united these programs—so diverse yet so committed to the cause of the street child—was a major design constraint with little guidance on what impacts (expected and unexpected effects) to look for. Lack of organized records of actions and accomplishments was another constraint. In the conventional sense, neither the dependent nor the independent variables could be fully identified and described. The study would be a pioneering attempt to explore and describe a unified vision of these several hundred programs. It was a challenge to capture emotionally or politically sensitive data from stakeholders—without scaring away the street children like other aggressors, and without intimidating program staff and coordinators who often viewed evaluation as a technical instrument of hierarchical accountability rather than as a learning tool for program management. The situation called for nonreactive or unobtrusive methods and measures (Webb,

Campbell, Schwartz, & Sechrest, 1966) that would be less threatening than the more openly evaluative, conventional instruments like fixed-response questionnaires.

Naturalistic-responsive evaluation (Guba & Lincoln, 1985) was the best fit for unveiling street children program realities because of (a) the emphasis on discovering rather than verifying the truth, (b) permitting designs to emerge from experience rather than working from preordinate designs, and (c) recognizing the value of rich, qualitative data captured through participant observation. Often, the instrument is the observer himself or herself, or the *human instrument* (Stake, 1975). Thus, the instruments of choice *par excellence* were the three evaluators themselves. They would observe selected programs with a systematic scheme, for which they would interact with (a) the street children under observation; (b) key informants such as program coordinators and street educators, as well as community members with first-hand knowledge of what was happening around the children; and (c) any program documents or records available for consulting, including newspapers.

Street Evaluators

The evaluators soon recognized that their encounters with the program and those of the street educators were similar—including the need for initial "courtship" with the children in order to establish rapport and elicit authentic responses. Indeed, Freirean principles that guided street educator interactions and dialoguing with children were also valid for evaluator interactions with the children. With the onus thus placed on them, the evaluators exclaimed: "Street evaluators!—That is what we will be!" And so it was. The evaluation team had encountered a common ground with the street children programs and began to gain contextual relevance.

As human instruments, they would act collectively and individually as participant observers in the selected programs, using a variety of unobtrusive techniques (as described in the next section), often improvised on the hour. They would be open to any needed nonparticipant observations, such as observing the program environment, recording critical incidents, or consulting documents. These would be used for cross-checking data. All this was to ensure that responses drawn in a sensitive environment were in fact authentic and relevant. Additionally, rigor (credibility) was to be ensured by constantly cross checking data through triangulation (Guba & Lincoln, 1985, pp. 106–107). Each evaluator would draw data from at least two different methods or sources and check them against each other. This would be further triangulated among the evaluators themselves in a next step. The intent was to infuse enlightened subjectivity into the evaluative process in accordance with the Freirean principle of valuing and integrating the objective and subjective.

New Directions for Evaluation • DOI: 10.1002/ev

Data Collection—Phase I: Generating Program Impact Indicators

The evaluators decided to identify impact indicators through field observation of street children behavior, rather than derive them from theory. This bottom-up approach was both fitting and feasible within the naturalistic design and consistent with Freirean pedagogy. Through the Alternative Programs project, the evaluators gained access to free and open encounters with street children at the national congress of street children in Brasilia in May 1986, which drew some 400 young representatives of street children programs from all parts of Brazil (National Commission for Street Boys and Girls Movement, 1986). As invited friends of the street educators, the evaluators easily became participant observers in events of the meeting and gained confidence of the participating children, mingling freely with them during activities and breaks. Through informal chats they prompted children to talk, to tell stories and talk about the program and also about other children. Understanding impact as "change of behavior," the evaluators focused on obtaining "clues" about what ideas and behaviors might indicate possible changes induced by the program. Their interactions were always centered on getting responses to five questions:

1. What program are you in (name and location)?
2. In what way has the program changed you?
3. What in the program has caused you to change in this way?
4. What do you intend to do from now on, and when you grow up?
5. What message would you give to children who are not in a program like yours?

Responses were noted unobtrusively by each evaluator as much as possible. Usually each evaluator worked alone, but sometimes they worked in pairs so that one could observe the interview by sitting aside and noting nonverbal behaviors. Sometimes an excited child or two would allow themselves to be recorded on audio-tape. Notes were taken at a distance; the children's behavior in their natural habitat was observed. For example, children organized their own lunchtime activities with no adult supervision and lined up in order, suggesting organizational ability, independence, and respect for others. Children spontaneously cleaned up the place after meeting, without being told, suggesting social responsibility. The evaluators triangulated their independent observations at various opportunities during the day, arriving at joint conclusions about what indicators were suggested by clues.

Changes that seemed to have occurred mostly suggested psycho-social growth and included attitudes, values, and skills. Analysis of these perceptions generated an initial list of 46 impact indicators. The evaluation team perceived a natural pattern in the spread of the indicators, which suggested their grouping into four categories: social skills, career skills, personal growth, and moral values. The indicators thus categorized comprised an initial bank of indicators, which would be the basis for identifying impacts in Phase II—systematic observation of selected programs. The indicator bank was deliberately left "open" to accommodate any new indicators possibly detected during program observations.

Based on the results of Phase I, the following evaluation questions were framed to guide the observation of programs to detect impacts.

Evaluation Questions

Overall question. What is the impact of the alternative service programs on street children?
Specific questions. As a result of their experience in the program, what changes are occurring in the children's social skills, career (job) skills, personal (individual) growth, and moral values?

Data Collection—Phase II: Detecting Impacts by Observing Programs

Sample

Eleven street children programs were selected for study from all over Brazil; the programs were chosen to reflect regional, philosophical, organizational, and methodological diversity. Program officials all freely volunteered their programs to participate in the evaluation. The programs varied in experience, the oldest program had been in operation for 15 years, the youngest only 2 years. The included programs served the needs of children "of the street," who lived there and others that cared for the children "on the street," working there for a living.

Procedures

The evaluators visited each of the 11 programs by traveling to the location as a team, and spending at least two days of intense, systematic observations, sometimes staying over a third day. They arrived with the indicator bank in hand, having made a checklist of them against which to make observations. However, not all indicators in the bank would be relevant to a specific program, so the first task was to identify those that seemed to relate to the program. Then, with specific indicators on the checklist, evidence of impact would be gathered with respect to each specific indicator. Accordingly, the first day was reserved for an "immersion" in the program to get a sense of the totality of it through free observations, shedding personal biases and seeing the program with new eyes. The clues to possible impacts should enable the evaluators to identify and draw a set of indicators from the indicator bank that were relevant to the program. The second day was then

spent on doing more directed observations focused on the identified indicators. The observation scheme was more structured, and the intent was to
determine whether the impacts suggested during immersion were changes
that really occurred in children as a result of their experience in the program. The process on both days was naturalistic and included continuous
data triangulation, as detailed below.

Initial Immersion in the Program

Similar to their observations made in Phase I, the evaluators collected multiple clues about possible impacts—talking to children and key informants
(street educators and community members that came in) and freely observing critical incidents (unusual or remarkable occurrences) and activities.
They sensed the totality of the program, its challenges, history, objectives,
and frustrations. Through dialogues, observation, play, dramatization, and
free observations of children, and in the comments of the street educators
and program staff, many clues to possible impacts of the specific program
emerged. Some examples follow. An exhaustive list may be found in the full
report (Penna-Firme et al, 1987).

Children's statements.

"We don't have to run away from here, because here we are free" (relevant
indicator—appreciation of the program).
"We worked out the problem with dialogue and not with our fists" (relevant
indicator—nonviolent problem solving).
"With our Cooperative we earn more and spend less" (relevant indicator—
efficient use of earnings).

Critical incidents.

A boy of more or less 13 years old arrives at the program locale bringing a
girl of the same age whom he had recruited on the street to join his work
group (consideration for others).
Two boys in charge of the print shop of the program surprise the evaluators
by offering them their business card (printed by them) with information
about their small private printing business established in their neighbor-
hood. They guarantee rapid and efficient service (initiative for work).

Observation of behavior in their natural environment.

Children meet in an assembly to draw up rules of the house, which are hung
on the wall (relevant indicator—democratic participation).
A boy, called "professor" by the others, voluntarily takes on the role of ori-
enting newcomers to the program" (relevant indicator—solidarity with
one's own class).

Comments volunteered by street educators and volunteer staff working with the children.

"The boys used to be very violent when they played; now they are more peaceful" (a personal growth indicator).
"They already had leadership quality when they entered, but here they learned to use it constructively" (a social skills indicator).
"The older boys don't want to be shoe-shine boys any more, and are asking for better jobs" (a job skills indicator).
"Destructive acts have diminished considerably" (a personal growth indicator).
"The children are concerned with the situation of comrades who are infractors" (a moral values indicator).

At the end of the day, the evaluators triangulated their notes and identified the indicators that were most relevant to the specific program. This resulted in a cohesive common version of the program and its objectives, with appropriate indicators from the preliminary bank. It also resulted in a refined version of the bank of indicators with the addition of newly emerged indicators.

Direct Observation in the Programs

Two major challenges had to be overcome before focused observation could be made. Unlike in immersion, the evaluators looked for evidences to determine if the impacts suggested during immersion were in fact program effects. The first challenge was to assess the degree or intensity of impact in some way for recording the behavioral evidences against each indicator on the scoring sheet. Most indicators were psycho-social, referring to attitudes and value development and thus were less amenable to concrete measuring. The evaluators decided to use Bloom's taxonomy in the affective domain (Krathwohl, Bloom, & Masia, 1964) and chose its two most observable stages as their criteria for scoring. These were "valuing" and "characterizing"—the third and fifth stages, respectively. A child in the valuing stage was expected to manifest adoption of a value, even if temporarily (for example, honesty in selling his merchandise). This case was noted as "some signs (SS)" of impact regarding that particular indicator. Another child might be in the fifth stage, holding on to a value more permanently as a habit and being characterized by it (for example, the child defends honesty and leads others to be honest); this case was registered as "marked (M)" impact. Depending on what stage most of the children seemed to be, the program itself was considered having an impact of SS or M with respect to each indicator. When no evidence showed up, it was noted as "not evident."
A second major challenge was to obtain evidence of impact or "pre–post" changes despite a lack of baseline data. The evaluators were con-

stantly aware of this constraint during interactions with children and key informants inside or outside the program, and they always framed their questions in terms of "changes"—asking "how were you (or your friends) different before coming into the program"? It often called for spur-of-the-moment thinking. A couple of examples follow.

Example 1. Pouring rain outside the cathedral building held a large group of children as a captive audience. A small group started conversing with one of the evaluators. Suddenly one boy started to communicate through mime. Praising the boy on his talent, the evaluator encouraged the child to dramatize the status of his friends before, during, and after their participation in the program—in three acts. Inspired by the mime, another boy spontaneously offered an oral interpretation of the meaning of the mime. Together, and unaware, the two had revealed changes (and perhaps program impact) according to their own perception. A second evaluator quietly took notes on the nonverbal gestures and reactions of other children around, their head nods, and other signs of agreement with what the mime described. The third evaluator walked around the group of children and observed them from different angles and triangulated the information later with the first two evaluators.

Example 2. During conversations with street children in a downtown plaza where they habitually hung out, one of the evaluators gave hand and finger puppets to a couple of children, who used the puppets to tell their life stories and describe their own situations. They were encouraged to assume various roles such as mother, boy, girl, policeman, or program staff. It brought out rich expression of the children's problems and the program's solutions. It also revealed changes and comparison between the plaza children who were in programs and those who were not.

Participant Observation

Many observational methods and techniques naturally emerged as the evaluators freely interacted in a *participant observer* role. They welcomed opportunities to take part in role plays, or coordinate a group session, or to teach how to do a calculation at the request of the children. Note-taking was in these cases done at the end. Natural settings like this opened up further opportunities for unobtrusive observation, such as

1. *Drawing and painting activities* in the program's leisure moments. Personality traits like enthusiasm, ability to concentrate for long periods, free and surprisingly smooth in composition and color, with no hint of personalities marked by violence, were evident. Also evident were qualities of sensitivity and leadership combined with insecurity, a longing for affection, and traces of anxiety and shyness.
2. *Observation of whole settings*, capturing dynamics of relationships of children among themselves and with program staff, which revealed

affectivity, reduced violence, as well as critical thinking and aspirations.

3. *Life stories* that evidenced changes resulting from program participation, as revealed through a retrospective view of the children, as recounted by themselves.

4. *Informal conversations*, when children talked naturally and openly about the program, an opportunity for the evaluators to bring up certain themes in function of the indicators.

5. *Visits to special settings*—such as a cooperative or a crafts workshop or a program event—revealed children's job skills and attitudes including the ability to organize and administer their cooperative, spontaneous cooperation to maintain the locale, sharing small space without conflict.

Additionally, children showed critical thinking and social skills, by discussing current social and political topics related to their situation, resolving their differences amicably in meetings, and talking to the visiting evaluators intelligently about children's rights in context of an upcoming national constitutional convention.

In addition to participant observation, formal, yet congenial and open-ended, interviews were used to obtain information from key informants including program staff, community people, and former program participants. Program documents were also consulted and discussed to obtain a more complete picture of the program's underlying philosophy, successes, and difficulties. Key informant statements were especially helpful in capturing changes as perceived by them as evidences of impact, as shown in the examples below.

For all observations made using the different techniques, each evaluator noted them on the checklist against the appropriate indicators. The behaviors were not "clues," but actual changes or pieces of evidences of impact with respect to the particular indicator. Such data, drawn from at least two different methods or sources, permitted the evaluator to confirm the impact.

Sample statements and comments by street educators, volunteers, and other program staff.

"The children cooperate spontaneously in cleaning, painting, and repairing the program locale" (change in social skills, with respect to the indicator: cooperation).

"The children drastically reduce their violent behavior toward each other, adult staff, and the general environment" (change in social skills, with respect to the indicator resolving problem without violence).

"The children correctly account for the sale of their products" (change in career skills, with respect to the indicator efficient use of earnings).

"The children arrive on time to discharge their responsibilities in the program" (change in career skills, with respect to the indicator: responsibility on the job).
"The children speak about themselves in positive terms" (change in personal/individual growth, with respect to the indicator self-esteem).
"The children criticize any form of repression and consider themselves deserving of good treatment" (change in personal/individual growth, with respect to the indicator: Critical thinking).
"The children defend their rights and draw up a code of conduct for the program" (change in moral values with respect to the indicator sense of justice).
"The children participate voluntarily and respectfully in religious services" (change in mal values with respect to the indicator spirituality).

Triangulation

At the end of the second day, the evaluators further triangulated their conclusions and perceptions of impact among one another. Before leaving the program and moving on to the next site, the evaluators met with the program coordinator to report and discuss the results to validate their own perceptions against the program's. This was an added precaution to preserve data authenticity. Notably, the coordinators were in agreement with most perceptions. Any minor concerns were noted for future checks in other programs.

The foregoing steps were repeated in each program, visiting them in sequence. Between two visits, the impacts for each program were consolidated by double triangulation—first individually on the evaluator level, and next collectively on the team level. Additionally, the preliminary indicator bank was expanded by adding the newly emerged indicators. Also, the systematic scheme itself was reviewed and refined for the subsequent visit—adding, dropping, or modifying steps.

Results

Impacts and Program Profiles

The analyses resulted in an overview of impacts across all programs. Moderate to high impacts were occurring in the street children, ranging between relative values of 58% and 70%. Most impacts were occurring in social skills, followed by moral values, job skills, and personal growth, in that order. This made sense when checked against what kind of learning opportunities were available in the activities of these programs that were visited (Penna-Firme et al., 1987).

However, not all programs individually replicated this result. This was seen in their individual program profiles constructed by using their impact scores. The impacts seemed to follow a pattern that clustered programs into two distinct groups, six in the first group and five in the second. The evaluators called these Type 1 and Type 2 programs and examined other related data that explained these differences. It appeared that the Type 1 programs were those that served children working "on the street," and Type 2 programs served the needier, homeless children "of the street."

The difference above explained why the Type 1 cluster had higher impacts than did the Type 2 cluster—social skills (81% vs. 52%), job skills (79% vs. 40%), moral values (74% vs. 53%), and personal growth (63% vs. 51%). Additionally, Type 1 programs had the least impact on personal growth of children, and Type 2 had least impact on job skills of children. Evidently, the latter programs had a longer and harder path of courtship, working on children's basic issues of personal growth and civic attitudes, before the children were ready for any kind of job training. The Type 1 programs, on the other hand, could spend less effort on these basic issues and could attract children for job training activities relatively quickly. Indeed, in some of the Type 1 programs, children were producing arts and crafts of exportable quality. It should be noted that Type 1 programs were also older than their Type 2 counterparts. To reiterate, all impact values across both types were either high or moderate, and there were no low impacts.

A Systematic Methodology for Ongoing Evaluation of the Programs

Emergent from the naturalistic–responsive evaluation process was also a methodology for collecting and compiling authentic and credible data for continuous program monitoring and improvement. Having been tested and refined by passing through the 11 programs, the study produced a method relevant to street children programs and hence valuable to program coordinators and to the alternative service programs project at UNICEF.

Discussion and Conclusions

The Impact of Evaluation on Stakeholders

The results were compiled and disseminated to major stakeholders in various formats. Oral presentations were made before preparing the final report—first to UNICEF and the Alternative Service Programs project in Brasilia, and then to the representatives of the 11 programs in Rio de Janeiro in a 2-day seminar. The programs showed great enthusiasm and receptivity to the evaluators' efforts and results, and appreciated both the bank of indicators and the evaluation methodology as valuable pedagogical tools. Interestingly, when the evaluators pointed out their use as self-evaluation tools, they surprised the evaluators by saying that they would rather be externally evaluated by the evaluators! This was reassuring, in a climate where evaluation was notorious as an intimidator, and it attested to the credibility of this evaluation and its value for these stakeholders. The highlight of the meeting occurred when they validated the impact profiles of the 11 programs as accurate. They easily identified themselves in the anonymous and coded graph, exclaiming "there I am, that is me, program B is me, of course!!" and so on. They also confirmed, in a single voice, that the difference between the Type 1 and Type 2 programs was in fact due to the different clientele posing different challenges. Overall, the meeting validated the naturalistic study methods and the sense of trust it had engendered, and it acknowledged that the evaluation had been responsive to their concerns.

UNICEF received a comprehensive written report from the evaluators and published the study (Penna-Firme et al., 1990). In revisiting the evaluation experience in this chapter, the intent is to highlight the validity of Freire's ideas for evaluative thinking in the context, as well as to share the methodological aspects of special interest to the evaluation community and to professionals in allied disciplines.

Lessons Learned/Taught

Freire maintained that *one cannot teach without learning, nor learn without teaching*. The two acts are simultaneous, and there is knowledge exchange.

What did the evaluators learn? First and foremost, they learned that naturalistic–responsive methods are both feasible and effective in an emotionally and politically sensitive context. Different from earlier evaluations the team had conducted, this was an "experientially-arrived-at" conclusion, based on participation and knowledge exchange in the context. Credible data were collected, leading to credible results. If this is a criterion of degree of effectiveness, the process can also said to be cost effective, making qualitative data collection worth the expense—not always to shy away from.

For the evaluators, learning to be *human instruments* was crucial, which in the study context, meant practice of Freirean principles. Fundamentally it meant openness. On one level it required a certain "value reorientation" to be able to practice empathy and sensitivity in interactions with people. Curiously, this implied being nonjudgmental, which the evaluators found to be a parallel to the *neutral* posture in the scientific sense—however, it meant to be "close and caring," not "cold and distant."

On another level, Freirean openness meant critical thinking. The evaluators learned to question their methodological choices every step of the way, devising context-appropriate methods and measures without compromising data quality, but in fact enhancing it through creativity. How to make up for lack of baseline data? How to measure what you must, instead of measuring only what you can? Concretely, how to quantify and assess affective behavior? The evaluators learned to face the challenge of making human subjectivity an asset rather than a liability, by combining critical thinking with creativity for making enlightened choices. In this sense, contextual constraints often turned into opportunities. As one of the evaluators put it, they found wisdom in following a "street methodology" and let go of a "strict methodology." The evaluators learned, also, to be a cohesive team,

NEW DIRECTIONS FOR EVALUATION • DOI: 10.1002/ev

sharing the above qualities—diverse and critical in their inputs, but always united by the context values—much needed for triangulations.

What Did the Evaluators Teach? What Knowledge Did They Impart?

Obviously, the key outputs—the impacts, the indicator bank, and the evaluation methodology scheme—all provided new knowledge to stakeholders. Less obvious, but perhaps the most valuable teaching, especially on the level of the program staff, as well as street children, was the knowledge that evaluation is a friend, not a foe; that evaluators can be trusted as human beings and as professionals; that data serve a common cause, and are not always used for individual exploitation.

Postscript

In closing, it should be noted that, while much more remains to be done for the street child in the Brazilian scene, the popular national movement in favor of children and adolescents, catalyzed by UNICEF's Alternative Services project in the 1980s, led to the historic creation of the Statute of Children and Adolescents (Brasil, 1990, Lei Federal 8069/90). It introduced new rights for the young Brazilian population, in a radically innovative approach that embraced the UN's doctrine of full protection based on the Declaration of Children's rights (Gomes da Costa, 1993). What is lacking is the full implementation of this federal law, to support an improved social and educational context in which young people are growing up. However, street children programs have multiplied since and have gone on from being "alternatives" to "alteratives"—they are change-oriented, networking with schools and various social organizations. A general awareness of the problem pervades the country. And one can see Freire's influence implicit in the practice of these programs. The hope is that, with the imprints of this great Brazilian educator, the profession of street educator will one day disappear, and street children will as well. Who knows, the expression "the place of the child is in the school" may one day be re-phrased as "the place of the school is in the child"? Then, the child will be truly a national priority, and indeed, a universal priority. In the meantime, as Paulo Freire used to say, "To do tomorrow what is impossible today, we need to do today what is possible today."

References

Brasil. (1990). Estatuto da Criança e do Adolescente—Lei 8069/90. Brasília, DF.
Douglas, J. D. (1976). *Investigative social research*. Beverly Hills, CA: Sage.
Espert, F., & Myers, W. (1988). *Situation analysis. Latin America and the Caribbean Regional Programme* (Children in Especially Difficult Circumstances Outreach Series, No. 1). Bogota, Columbia: UNICEF.
Freire, P. (2000). *Educação como prática da liberdade*. Rio de Janeiro, Brazil: Paz e Terra.

Freire, P. (2005). *Pedadgogia do oprimido* (42nd ed.). Rio de Janeiro, Brazil: Paz e Terra.

Freire, P. (2013). *Pedadgogy of the oppressed* [translated from Portuguese (Freire, 1970) with introduction by Donaldo Macedo (2000)] (30th anniversary edition). New York, NY: Bloomsbury.

Freire, P. (2014). *Pedagogy of hope—Reliving pedagogy of the oppressed* (Robert R. Barr, Trans.). New York, NY: Bloomsbury.

Gomes da Costa, A. C. (1993). *É possível mudar—A criança, o adolescente e a Política Social do Município/Séie Direitos da Criança, 1.* São Paulo, Brazil: Malheiros, Ltda.

Guba, E., & Lincoln, Y. S. (1985). *Effective evaluation.* San Francisco, CA: Jossey-Bass.

Krathwohl, D. R., Bloom, B. S., & Masia, B. B. (1964). Taxonomy of educational objectives: The classification of educational goals. *Handbook II: The affective domain.* New York, NY: David McKay.

Myers, W. (Ed.). (1988). *Protecting working children.* London, United Kingdom: Zed Books Ltd./UNICEF.

National Commission for the Street Boys and Girls Movement. (1986, May 28). *The first national meeting of the boys and girls of the street—Results of mini-plenary sessions* [Report of the Commission (in Portuguese)]. Brasilia: National Commission.

Penna-Firme, T., Tijiboy, J. A., & Stone, V. I. (1987). *An evaluation of the impact of alternative service programs on street children* (John Stone, Trans.) (Unpublished research report). Brasilia: UNICEF.

Penna-Firme, T., Tijiboy, J. A., & Stone, V. I. (1991). The generation and observation of evaluation indicators of the psycho-social development of participants in programs for street children. In W. Myers (Ed.), *Protecting working children (Chap. 5).* London, United Kingdom: Zed Books Ltd./UNICEF.

Stake, R. E. (1975). *Evaluating the arts in education: a responsive apparoach.* Columbus, OH: Charles E. Merrill.

Swift, A. (1991). Brazil: The fight for childhood in the city. *Innocenti Studies.* Florence, Italy: UNICEF.

UNICEF. (1987). *Paulo Freire and the street educators—An analytical approach* (Children in Especially Difficult Circumstances Outreach Series, No. 1). Bogota, Columbia: UNICEF.

UNICEF/MPAS-Ministério da Previdência e Assistência Social. (n.d.). *O que é o projeto.* Rio de Janeiro, Brazil: Projeto Alternativas de Atendimento a Meninos de Rua.

Webb, E., Campbell, D. T., Schwartz, R., & Sechrest, L. (1966). *Unobtrusive measures: Nonreactive research in the social sciences.* Chicago, IL: Rand McNally.

Worthen, B. R., & Sanders, J. R. (1973). *Educational evaluation: Theory and practice.* Belmont, CA: Wadsworth.

THEREZA PENNA FIRME *is an educator and psychologist specializing in evaluation both by academic training and professional practice, has taught extensively at primary, secondary, and higher education levels in Brazil, and currently coordinates the Evaluation Center at the CESGRANRIO Foundation and is the evaluation consultant for the Roberto Marinho Foundation, both in Brazil.*

VATHSALA I. STONE, *with 40 years of experience as an evaluation professional in national and international contexts, including 17 years spent in Brazil, currently directs research and evaluation at the University of Buffalo's Center for Assistive Technology.*

NEW DIRECTIONS FOR EVALUATION • DOI: 10.1002/ev

Patton, M. Q. (2017). Pedagogical principles of evaluation: Interpreting Freire. In M. Q. Patton (Ed.), *Pedagogy of Evaluation. New Directions for Evaluation, 155*, 49–77.

3

Pedagogical Principles of Evaluation: Interpreting Freire

Michael Quinn Patton iD

Abstract

Pedagogy of evaluation entails examining how and what evaluation teaches. Embedded in different evaluation approaches are varying assumptions, values, premises, priorities, sense-making processes, and principles. Elucidating and illuminating principles is fundamental to identifying and understanding a pedagogy of evaluation. Ten pedagogical principles from Paulo Freire's writings are identified and explained. Each principle is then examined for its relevance to a critical pedagogy of evaluation for evaluation theory and practice today and looking forward. Freire understood and taught us that all interactions between and among people are pedagogical, something is always being taught, conveyed, and proselytized. Extending this insight to evaluation, Freire's work reminds us that all evaluation approaches constitute a pedagogy of some kind. What any particular evaluation teaches and how it is taught varies, but evaluation is inherently and predominantly a pedagogical interaction. This leads to the concluding question: What is your pedagogy of evaluation? © 2017 Wiley Periodicals, Inc., and the American Evaluation Association.

A Principles-Focused Pedagogy of Evaluation

*P*edagogy of evaluation entails examining how and what evaluation teaches. Embedded in different evaluation approaches are varying assumptions, values, premises, priorities, sense-making processes, and *principles*. I'm going to focus on principles as fundamental to a pedagogy of evaluation. Those who participate in an evaluation are experiencing sometimes explicit, more often implicit and tacit, *pedagogical principles*. Principles inform and guide decision making. They do so by telling us where to focus our attention and how to act. For example, goal-based evaluation is derived from the principle that setting goals increases effectiveness, which tells us to focus on and measure goal attainment. Theory-driven evaluation is based on the principle that interventions are more likely to be effective if based on a theory of change and thereby tells us to focus on and assess program theory. Utilization-focused evaluation is based on the principle that identifying and working with intended users on intended uses will enhance use. Developmental evaluation is grounded in complexity theory, which focuses our attention on the principle of emergence which directs us to be open and agile in capturing emergent outcomes in complex dynamic situations. This chapter will identify and elucidate the pedagogical principles of Paulo Freire and examine their implications for evaluation thereby illuminating a Freirean pedagogy of evaluation. This is a form of *principles-focused evaluation* (Patton, 2017).

Principles-focused evaluation examines (a) whether principles are clear, meaningful, and actionable, and if so (b) whether they are actually being followed and, if so (c) whether they are leading to desired results. Principles are derived from experience, expertise, values, and research. They operate at different levels. They can guide individual, program, policy, organizational, and community choices and actions. There are design principles, relationship principles, principles of professional practice, philanthropic principles, accountability principles, policy-making principles, sustainability principles, research principles, and so forth and so on, because every arena of human endeavor has generated guiding principles. By identifying Freirean pedagogical principles and evaluating their relevance and applicability to evaluation, I hope to illustrate how principles make explicit the pedagogy embedded in a particular evaluation approach. That process can then be used to illuminate the pedagogy of any evaluation.

Principles-focused evaluation informs choices about which principles are appropriate for what purposes in which contexts, helping to navigate the treacherous terrain of conflicting guidance and competing advice. What principles work for what situations with what results is an evaluation question. Thus, from an evaluation perspective, principles are hypotheses, not truths. They may or may not work. They may or may not be followed. They may or may not lead to desired outcomes. Whether they work, whether they are followed, and whether they yield desired outcomes are subject to evaluation.

I've extracted 10 pedagogical principles from Freire's writings. I'll explain each principle and its relevance for a critical pedagogy of evaluation. I'll begin by summarizing an evaluation scenario from *Pedagogy of the Oppressed* and then extract Freire's principles from that example and examine their relevance for evaluation today and looking forward. I will quote extensively from Freire to provide a sense of his language and perspective. The scenario and all quotations are from *Pedagogy of the Oppressed* (Freire, 1970) unless otherwise noted.

Freire's Evaluation Engagement Process

What follows is Freire's example of his pedagogy of the oppressed undergirded by critical evaluative thinking. Here's the scenario: A plan is to be developed and implemented for adult education in a peasant area with high illiteracy. The process begins with a participatory situation analysis facilitated by "investigators." The investigators hold an informal meeting in the area where the literacy campaign is to take place. During this initial meeting with local people they explain what they propose to do and that "the investigation will be impossible without a relation of mutual understanding and trust" (p. 110). Volunteers are recruited at this meeting to serve as assistants in gathering data about the life of the area. Together the investigators and volunteers develop "a critical perception of the world, which implies a correct method of approaching reality in order to unveil it. And critical perception cannot be imposed. Thus, from the very beginning, thematic investigation is expressed as an educational pursuit, as cultural action" (p. 111):

> The inquiry observes people living life and engages in informal conversations with them. They register everything in their notebooks, including apparently unimportant items: the way the people talk, their style of life, their behavior at church and at work. They record the idioms of the people: their expressions, their vocabulary, and their syntax (not their incorrect pronunciation, but rather the way they construct their thought).

> It is essential that the investigators observe the area under varying circumstances: labor in the fields, meetings of a local association (noting the behavior of the participants, the language used, and the relations between the officers and the members), the role played by women and by young people, leisure hours, games and sports, conversations with people in their homes (noting examples of husband–wife and parent–child relationships). No activity must escape the attention of the investigators during the initial survey of the area. (pp. 111–112)

The process then moves from data to interpretation, which means engaging in evaluation.

> After each observation visit, the investigator should draw up a brief report to be discussed by the entire team, in order to evaluate the preliminary findings of both the professional investigators and the local assistants. To facilitate the participation of the assistants, the evaluation meetings should be held in the area itself. (p. 112)

During these "evaluation meetings" each person reports "how he perceived or felt a certain occurrence or situation." In so doing, Freire explains, participants in the inquiry challenge each other "by re-presenting to them the same reality upon which they have themselves been intent. At this moment they 're-consider,' through the 'considerations' of others, their own previous 'consideration.'" Thus "the analysis of reality" made by each individual "sends them all back, dialogically, to the disjoined whole which once more becomes a totality evoking a new analysis by the investigators, following which a new evaluative and critical meeting will be held. Representatives of the inhabitants participate in all activities as members of the investigating team" (p. 112).

The initial investigation focuses on uncovering and understanding contradictions of consciousness among the people being studied. However, Freire cautions: "the fact that the investigators may in the first stage of the investigation approximately apprehend the complex of contradictions does not authorize them to begin to structure the program content of educational action. This perception of reality is still their own, not that of the people" (p. 114). Instead, a second stage of inquiry is initiated to further investigate these contradictions, "always acting as a team." The contradictions identified must be familiar to the participants in the inquiry. "It is inadmissible ... to present pictures of reality unfamiliar to the participants" because the purpose is for "individuals analyzing their own reality to become aware of their prior, distorted perceptions and thereby to have a new perception of that reality." Through this inquiry the participants "make explicit their 'real consciousness' of the world. As they do this, they begin to see how they themselves acted while actually experiencing the situation they are now analyzing, and thus reach a 'perception of their previous perception'" (p. 114).

By achieving this awareness, they come to perceive reality differently; by broadening the horizon of their perception, they discover more easily in their "background awareness" the dialectical relations between the two dimensions of reality.

By stimulating "perception of the previous perception" and "knowledge of the previous knowledge," decoding stimulates the appearance of a new perception and the development of new knowledge. The new perception and knowledge are systematically continued with the inauguration of the educational plan, which transforms the untested feasibility into testing action, as potential consciousness supersedes real consciousness." (p. 115)

Freire reports having learned with colleagues that the people in communities only become deeply interested and engaged when the inquiry related "directly to their felt needs. Any deviation ... produced silence and indifference" (p. 116). With further work, Freire and colleagues developed a pedagogy of critical consciousness that moved beyond mere needs identification to perceiving the *causes* of their needs. Therein lies the emergence of critical consciousness.

> In one of the thematic investigations carried out in Santiago, a group of tenement residents discussed a scene showing a drunken man walking on the street and three young men conversing on the corner. The group participants commented that "the only one there who is productive and useful to his country is the spouse who is returning home after working all day for low wages and who is worried about his family because he can't take care of their needs. He is the only worker. He is a decent worker and a souse like us." ... [I]n their comments on the codification of an existential situation they could recognize, and in which they could recognize themselves, they said what they really felt... .

> In contrast, imagine the failure of a moralistic educator sermonizing against alcoholism and presenting as an example of virtue something which for these men is not a manifestation of virtue. In this and in other cases, the only sound procedure is the *conscientizaciio* of the situation, which should be attempted from the start of the thematic investigation. (pp. 118–119)

Freire provides much more detail about how to move from inquiry to reflection to action while evaluating each step along the way and using what is learned in each action step to frame the next inquiry cycle, thereby deepening critical consciousness of the local people involved throughout the ongoing pedagogical journey.

Keep in mind that in this scenario Freire is describing his pedagogical approach of working with nonliterate poor people before evaluation had emerged as a formal field of professional practice.

Freirean Principles

There is no definitive list of Freirean principles. Different analysts, including the authors in this volume, drawing on and influenced by Freire's works emphasize different elements and articulate principles in varying ways. Thus, what follows are my interpretation of his principles with an eye toward particular influences on and relevance for evaluation.

Principle 1. Use Evaluative Thinking to Open Up, Develop, and Nurture *Critical Consciousness*

> The conviction of the oppressed that they must fight for their liberation is not a gift bestowed by the revolutionary leadership, but the result of their own *conscientizaciio*. (Freire, 1970, p. 67)

Critical consciousness, or *conscientização* (Portuguese), refers to attaining a deep, meaningful, realistic, and reality-based understanding of one's world. This includes becoming aware of how one has been indoctrinated and conditioned to think in particular ways by those with power and wealth who control traditional educational outlets including schools, governmental agencies, media outlets, and the business world. Freire (1970) introduced the idea of *conscientização* in his book *Pedagogy of the Oppressed* to emphasize that ordinary people, especially the poor, are oppressed by false consciousness, having internalized the message that they are inferior, without value, incapable, and useless. A pedagogy of the oppressed raises consciousness about the nature, sources, and implications of oppression, which include dominant and domineering myths so as to escape control by those in power and come to act with freedom and consciousness as a self-determining and thoughtful human being. This realization empowers the oppressed to take action.

> The best starting point for such reflections is the unfinishedness of our human condition. It is in this consciousness that the very possibility of learning, of being educated, resides. It is our immersion in this consciousness that gives rise to a permanent movement of searching, of curious interrogation that leads us not only to an awareness of the world but also to a thorough, scientific knowledge of it. This permanent movement of searching creates a capacity for learning not only in order to adapt to the world, but especially to intervene, to re-create, and to transform it. All of this is evidence of our capacity for learning, for completing our incompleteness in a distinct way from that characteristic of other mammals or of plants. (Freire, 2001, pp. 66–67)

Evaluation relevance today

> We are distressed by underprivilege. We see gaps among privileged patrons and managers and staff and underprivileged participants and communities.... We are advocates of a democratic society. (Stake, 2004, pp. 103–107)

Pioneering evaluator Robert Stake's quote reeks of values. Pioneering evaluator Michael Scriven (2015) considers the transition from value-free social science to values-based evaluation the first great revolution in the transdiscipline of evaluation. Incorporating and judging value is the major purpose of evaluation, but evaluators have long struggled with how to do so. Schwandt has summarized the challenges succinctly and astutely.

> Debates have centered on how explicit an evaluator must be about the criteria employed for judgment.... Controversy is associated with the extent to which and the manner in which stakeholders (and which ones—managers, commissioners, beneficiaries?) are to be involved in determining criteria...and whether the evaluator per se is the person ultimately responsible for the judgment. Disagreement surrounds whether there ought to be a universal set of criteria (e.g. the OECD/DAC criteria of relevance, effectiveness, efficiency, impact, and sustainability for evaluating development assistance),

whether a particular criterion or set of criteria are always paramount (e.g. cultural responsiveness, gender-responsiveness, equity-focus), or whether criteria are always matters to be negotiated in particular settings. Equally troublesome is the fact of considerable disagreement on how best to deal with multiple criteria, the so-called aggregation or synthesis problem. And, finally, disputes surround both the applicability and the justification of various methods for valuing (e.g. determining impact via experiments; judging efficiency by means of cost-benefit techniques) in specific contexts. (Schwandt, 2015, p. 463–464)

Freire unequivocally believed that the criteria of the poor and oppressed should be ascendant, but for that to occur they would need to develop critical consciousness. Today, Freire's pedagogical influence is manifest in and is represented by two major and intersecting evaluation pedagogies: critical systems heuristics as a way of operationalizing critical consciousness and evaluative thinking as a core capacity to be developed in the process of conducting evaluations. Critical systems heuristics in evaluation design and implementation emphasizes explicit attention to power dynamics, taking into account diverse perspectives representing diverse values, and being explicit about critical boundary decisions.

Every evaluative inquiry is 'bounded' in the sense that particular facts and values bearing on determining the value of the intervention under consideration are either included or excluded from analysis. Certain criteria of performance, for example, are considered more or less relevant, and certain kinds of evidence of performance are considered more or less important. These boundaries or choices are not naturally given (e.g. as features of the context) but social (and personal) constructions that define what is to be taken as germane to the analysis of value. (Schwandt, 2015, p. 464)

Evaluative thinking as a form of critical consciousness is fundamental to House's (1977) conceptualization of evaluation dialogue involving argumentative interaction between the evaluator and stakeholders, "a dialogue in which they are free to employ their reasoning" (p. 48). It is by challenging evaluative premises the evaluator puts forth that "the nature of the evaluation as argumentation becomes apparent" (House, 1977, p. 8). Democratic deliberative evaluation (House, 2014; House & Howe, 2000) both requires critical consciousness and enhances the capacity to think critically.

Principle 2. Consciousness Resides in Communities of People, Not Just Individuals

When they [the oppressed] discover within themselves the yearning to be free, they perceive that this yearning can be transformed into reality only when the same yearning is aroused in their comrades. (p. 47)

NEW DIRECTIONS FOR EVALUATION • DOI: 10.1002/ev

The emergence and nurturing of critical consciousness is both a cultural and political activity and is therefore inherently a collective activity: *inquiry together.* Freire's pedagogy involves people together examining issues that are important to them and their situation, what he calls "thematics."

> [T]he investigation of thematics involves the investigation of the people's thinking —thinking which occurs only in and among people together seeking out reality. I cannot think *for others* or *without others,* nor can others think *for me.* Even if the people's thinking is superstitious or naive, it is only as they rethink their assumptions in action that they can change. (Freire, 1970, p. 108).

Evaluation relevance today

> In the long history of humankind (and animal kind, too) those who learned to collaborate and improvise most effectively have prevailed. Charles Darwin (1809–1882)

Participatory evaluation has become a major distinct approach to evaluation. The first participatory evaluation guidebooks were written by and for community development workers in Latin America and Africa. A collaborative group called Private Agencies Collaborating Together (1986) published one of the first guides to *Participatory Evaluation,* as well as a more general *Evaluation Sourcebook* (Pietro, 1983). Both remain relevant today. The guides include techniques for actively involving nonliterate people as active participants in evaluating the development efforts they experience. Those works acknowledge the influence of Freire.

Participatory, community-focused evaluation has been used with great success as part of international and community development efforts by a number of nongovernmental groups and private voluntary organizations in the Global South. International studies of development have demonstrated how participatory research can be a means of understanding and bridging diverse perspectives for responsive development (Better Evaluation, 2014; Mansuri & Vijayendra, 2012; Salmen & Kane, 2006). The processes of participation and collaboration have an impact on participants and collaborators quite beyond whatever findings or report they may produce by working together. In the process of participating in evaluation, participants are exposed to and have the opportunity to learn the logic of evidence-based inquiry and the discipline of evidentiary reasoning. Skills are acquired in problem identification, criteria specification, and data collection, analysis, and interpretation. Through acquisition of inquiry skills and ways of thinking, a collaborative inquiry process can have an impact beyond the findings generated from a particular study.

Moreover, people who participate in creating something tend to feel more ownership of what they have created and make more use of it.

New Directions for Evaluation • DOI: 10.1002/ev

Active participants in evaluation, therefore, are more likely to feel owner-ship not only of their findings but also of the inquiry process itself. Properly, sensitively, and authentically done, it becomes their process. Participants and collaborators can be community members, villagers, organizational workers, program staff, and/or program participants (e.g., clients, students, farmers). Sometimes administrators, funders, and others also participate, but the usual connotation is that the primary participants are "lower down" in the hierarchy—Freire's people. Participatory evaluation is bottom-up. The trick is to make sure that participation is genuine and authentic, not just token or rhetorical, especially in participative evaluation, where differ-ing political agendas often compete.

There are four distinct purposes for participatory evaluation: (a) the pragmatic purpose of increasing use of findings by those involved (Patton 2008); (b) the philosophical or methodological purpose of grounding data in participants' perspectives; (c) the political purpose of mobilizing for so-cial action, for example, empowerment evaluation (see Chapter 6 in this volume), or what is sometimes called "emancipatory" evaluation research (Cousins & Earl, 1995, p. 10); and (d) teaching inquiry logic and skills (Patton, 2015, p. 222). To achieve these evaluative purposes requires peo-ple in a community to inquire together actively. One community participant in such a process once told me: "We don't feel that we know something until we know it together." That is the essence of Freire's principle that *conscious-ness resides in communities of people, not just individuals.*

Principle 3. Critical Consciousness Pedagogy Must Be Interactive and Dialogical

Freire provides an extensive critique of what he calls the "banking" concept of education, in which teachers "deposit" information into students (Freire, 1970, p. 73). In contrast, the pedagogy of the oppressed must be interactive and dialogical.

> Those truly committed to liberation must reject the banking concept in its entirety, adopting instead a concept of women and men as conscious beings, and consciousness as consciousness intent upon the world. They must aban-don the educational goal of deposit-making and replace it with the posing of the problems of human beings in their relations with the world . . . .
>
> Liberating education consists in acts of cognition, not transferrals of infor-mation . . . . Dialogical relations indispensable to the capacity of cognitive actors to cooperate in perceiving the same cognizable object—are other-wise impossible . . . Through dialogue, the teacher-of-the-students and the students-of-the-teacher cease to exist and a new term emerges: teacher–student with students–teachers. The teacher is no longer merely the-one-who-teaches, but one who is himself taught in dialogue with the students, who in turn while being taught also teach. They become jointly responsible

for a process in which all grow … Here, no one teaches another, nor is anyone self-taught. People teach each other, mediated by the world, by the cogniz-able objects, which in banking education are "owned" by the teacher. (Freire, 1970, pp. 79–80)

Evaluation relevance today

To be human is to engage in interpersonal dynamics.

Inter: between.

Personal: people.

Dynamics: forces that produce activity and change.

Combining these definitions, interpersonal dynamics are the forces between people that lead to activity and change. Whenever and wherever people in-teract, these dynamics are at work. (King & Stevahn, 2013, p. 2)

This defining quotation from *Interactive Evaluation Practice* (King & Stevahn, 2013) makes explicit the connection between interactive evalua-tion approaches and social change. Likewise, democratic dialogic evalua-tion (House & Howe, 2000) presents both a rationale and a set of processes and methods to make dialogue among people with different perspectives and interests the cornerstone of evaluation in support of democracy. They have articulated three requirements for evaluation done in a way that sup-ports democracy: inclusion, dialogue, and deliberation. They worry about the power that derives from access to evaluation and the implications for society if only the powerful have such access.

We believe that the background conditions for evaluation should be explicitly democratic so that evaluation is tied to larger society by democratic princi-ples argued, debated, and accepted by the evaluation community. Evaluation is too important to society to be purchased by the highest bidder or appropri-ated by the most powerful interest. Evaluators should be self-conscious and deliberate about such matters … .

If we look beyond the conduct of individual studies by individual evaluators, we can see the outlines of evaluation as an influential societal institution, one that can be vital to the realization of democratic societies. Amid the claims and counterclaims of the mass media, amid public relations and advertising, amid the legions of those in our society who represent particular interests for pay, evaluation can be an institution that stands apart, reliable in the accuracy and integrity of its claims. But it needs a set of explicit democratic principles to guide its practices and test its intuitions. (House & Howe, 2000, p. 4)

Barry MacDonald (1987), influenced and inspired in part by Freire, was an early advocate of the democratic evaluation model. He argued that "the democratic evaluator" recognizes and supports value pluralism, with the consequence that the evaluator seeks to represent the full range of interests in the course of designing an evaluation. In this way, an evaluator can support an informed citizenry, the sine qua non of a strong democracy, by acting as an information broker between groups that want and need knowledge of one another. The democratic evaluator must make the methods and techniques of evaluation accessible to nonspecialists—that is, the general citizenry. MacDonald's democratic evaluator seeks to survey a range of interests by assuring confidentiality to sources, engaging in negotiation between interest groups, and making evaluation findings widely accessible. The guiding ethic is the public's right to know.

Saville Kushner (2000, 2016) has carried forward, deepened, and updated MacDonald's democratic evaluation model. He sees evaluation as a form of personal expression and political action, with a special obligation to be critics of those in power. He places at the center of evaluation the experiences of people in programs, the supposed beneficiaries, where, for Kushner, we will find the intersection of Politics (big P—Policy) and politics (small p—people). He uses case studies to capture the perspectives of real people—children and teachers and parents—and the realities of their lives in program settings as they experience those realities. He feels a special obligation to focus on, capture, report, and, therefore, honor the views of marginalized peoples. He calls this "personalizing evaluation," but the larger agenda is strengthening democracy. Consider these reflections on the need for evaluators and evaluations to address questions of social justice and the democratic contract:

> Where each social and educational program can be seen as a reaffirmation of the broad social contract (that is, are-confirmation of the bases of power, authority, social structure, etc.), each program evaluation is an opportunity to review its assumptions and consequences. This is commonly what we do at some level or another. All programs expose democracy and its failings; each program evaluation is an assessment of the effectiveness of democracy in tackling issues in the distribution of wealth and power and social goods [italics added]. Within the terms of the evaluation agreement, taking this level of analysis into some account, that is, renewing part of the social contract, is to act more authentically; to set aside the opportunity is to act more inauthentically, that is, to accept the fictions. (Kushner, 2000, pp. 32–33)

Writings on evaluation's role in supporting democratic processes reflect a significant shift in the nature of evaluation's real and potential contribution to strengthening democracy. A decade ago, the emphasis was all on increasing use of findings for enhanced decision making and program improvement and, therefore, making sure that findings reflected the diverse perspectives of multiple stakeholders, including the less powerful, through "inclusive evaluation" (Mertens, 1998, 1999) and genuinely engaging participants in programs, instead of just staff, administrators, and funders.

Although this thrust remains important, a parallel and reinforcing use of evaluation focuses on helping people learn to think and reason evaluatively and on how rendering such help can contribute to strengthening democracy over the long term, a Freirean vision that deserves elaboration.

Start with the premise that a healthy and strong democracy depends on an informed citizenry. A central contribution of policy research and evaluation, then, is to help ensure an informed electorate as well by disseminating findings, as well as to help the citizenry weigh evidence and think evaluatively. This involves thinking processes that must be learned. It is not enough to have trustworthy and accurate information (the informed part of the informed citizenry). People must also know how to use the information, that is, to weigh evidence, consider the inevitable contradictions and inconsistencies, articulate values, interpret findings, deal with complexity, and examine assumptions, to note but a few of the things meant by "thinking evaluatively." Moreover, in-depth democratic thinking includes political sophistication about the origins and implications of the categories, constructs, and concepts that shape what we experience as information and "knowledge" (Minnich, 2004), a core issue for Freire encompassed in his focus on critical consciousness.

Philosopher Hannah Arendt, also a contemporary of Freire, was especially attuned to this foundation of democracy. Having experienced Nazi totalitarianism, then having fled it, she devoted much of her life to studying it and its opposite, democracy. She believed that thinking thoughtfully in public deliberations and acting democratically were intertwined. Totalitarianism is built on and sustained by deceit and thought control. To resist efforts by the powerful to deceive and control thinking, Arendt (1968) believed that people needed to practice thinking. Toward that end, she developed "eight exercises in political thought." She wrote that "experience in thinking ... can be won, like all experience in doing something, only through practice, through exercises" (p. 4). From this point of view, might we consider every participatory research and evaluation inquiry as an opportunity for those involved to practice critical thinking and to increase critical consciousness? In this regard, we might aspire to have policy research, action research, participatory research, and collaborative evaluation do what Arendt hoped her exercises in political thought would do, namely, help us "to gain experience in how to think." Her exercises "do not contain prescriptions on what to think or which truths to hold" but, rather, on the act and process of thinking. For example, Arendt thought it important to help people think conceptually:

> to discover the real origins of original concepts in order to distill from them anew their original spirit which has so sadly evaporated from the very keywords of political language—such as freedom and justice, authority and reason, responsibility and virtue, power and glory—leaving behind empty shells. (Arendt, 1968, pp. 14–15)

Principle 4. Integrate Reflection and Action

Freire is strongly and eloquently critical of the juxtaposition of reflection and action as separate and distinct arenas of human experience. For him, reflection is aimed at action and action is the content of reflection. *Critical dialogue presupposes action.* At all stages of their liberation, the oppressed must see themselves as women and men engaged in the ontological and historical vocation of becoming more fully human. Reflection and action become imperative when one does not erroneously attempt to dichotomize the content of humanity from its historical forms.

The insistence that the oppressed engage in reflection on their concrete situation is not a call to armchair revolution. On the contrary, reflection—true reflection—leads to action. On the other hand, when the situation calls for action, that action will constitute an authentic praxis only if its consequences become the object of critical reflection (Freire, 1970, pp. 65–66).

Evaluation relevance today. *Reflective practice* has become a mainstay of professional development, action research, and learning organizations (Patton, 2008, 2011, 2015). Donald Schon (1983, 1987) popularized the concept of the reflective practitioner. What sets Freire apart was his pioneering and radical assertion that uneducated and nonliterate people could engage in, benefit from, become enlightened through, and bring about change as a result of reflection used to inform action. Social change toward social justice is the evidence that reflection-based inquiry has led to critical consciousness and that consciousness has informed action. Social justice evaluation, then, must examine both the quality of the community reflection process and the results of that process. This is the essence of *evaluating evaluation*, in this case, evaluating the extent to which social justice evaluation leads to greater social justice.

Principle 5. Value and Integrate the Objective and Subjective

Critical consciousness, reflection, and action must be grounded in objective reality that is subjectively experienced and understood.

> [T]he radical is never a subjectivist. For this individual the subjective aspect exists only in relation to the objective aspect (the concrete reality, which is the object of analysis). Subjectivity and objectivity thus join in a dialectical unity producing knowledge in solidarity with action, and vice versa. (Freire, 1970, p. 38)

At the core of critical consciousness is the "capacity to apprehend reality" (Freire, 1970/2000, p. 66). For Freire, poverty is a verifiable reality. Oppression is also a verifiable reality, not merely perception. Freire goes on at length to distinguish both intellectual and academic objectivism and subjectivism from commonsense objectivity and subjectivity as understood and experienced by ordinary people. Moreover, Freire asserts that any hoped for, alleged, or asserted transformation from oppression to liberation must be "objectively verified" (p. 50). Here are some illustrative and illuminative quotations.

> [O]ne cannot conceive of objectivity without subjectivity. Neither can exist without the other, nor can they be dichotomized. The separation of objectivity from subjectivity, the denial of the latter when analyzing reality or acting upon it, is objectivism. On the other hand, the denial of objectivity in analysis or action, resulting in a subjectivism which leads to solipsistic positions, denies action itself by denying objective reality. Neither objectivism nor subjectivism, nor yet psychologism is propounded here, but rather subjectivity and objectivity in constant dialectical relationship. (Freire, 2000, p. 50)

> Just as objective social reality exists not by chance, but as the product of human action, so it is not transformed by chance. If humankind produce social reality . . . , then transforming that reality is an historical task, a task for humanity. (Freire, 2000, p. 51)

> There would be no human action if there were no objective reality, no world to be the "not I" of the person and to challenge them; just as there would be no human action if humankind were not a "project," if he or she were not able to transcend himself or herself, if one were not able to perceive reality and understand it in order to transform it. (Freire, 2000, p. 53)

Evaluation relevance today. French philosopher Jean-Paul Sartre once observed that "words are loaded pistols." The words "objectivity" and "subjectivity" are bullets people arguing fire at each other. It's true that objectivity is held in high esteem. Science aspires to objectivity, and a primary reason why decision makers commission an evaluation is to get objective data from an independent source external to the program being evaluated. Yet, philosophers of science now typically doubt the possibility of anyone or any method being totally "objective." But subjectivity fares even worse. Even if acknowledged as inevitable, or valuable as a tool to understanding, subjectivity carries such negative connotations at such a deep level and for so many people that the very term can be an impediment to mutual understanding. Debate focused on objectivity versus subjectivity continues in evaluation and throughout science, but Freire offered an understanding of their connection and interdependence, a theme explored and enhanced by anthropologist and policy evaluator Michael Agar.

> "Subjective" versus "objective" no longer makes sense, since everyone involved is a subject ... Human Social Research is intersubjective ... built from encounters among subjects, including researchers who, like it or not, are also subjects. (Agar, 2013, pp. 108–109)

NEW DIRECTIONS FOR EVALUATION • DOI: 10.1002/ev

Eschewing both objectivity and subjectivity, intersubjectivity focuses on knowledge as socially constructed in human interactions. Evaluation and other forms of inquiry require "human social relationships in order to happen at all. They are intersubjective sciences. They require social relationships with those who support the science, those who do it, those who serve as subjects of it, and those who consume it" (Agar, 2013, p. 215).

> The difficult judgment call for the researcher is this: To some extent he or she should translate his or her own framework and jointly build a framework for communication with subjects of all those different types ... The bedrock of intersubjective research isn't to preach or to lecture, but rather to learn and to communicate the results, though not at the price of abandoning the core principles of the science. The pressure always exists to achieve a balance, and a researcher always has to make the call of how much and in what way to handle it.
>
> This fact has to be part of the science, not to mention a central part of training for human social researchers. How to navigate this ambiguous territory with professional integrity and product quality is a neglected topic ... . In my view, taking human social research out into the world makes it more difficult, more interesting, more intellectually challenging, and of higher moral value than it has ever been. (Agar, 2013, pp. 215–216)

Principle 6. Integrate Thinking and Emotion

Freire articulated a holistic and humanistic approach to dialogue that valued and integrated reason and emotions, especially in his last book, *Pedagogia da Autonomia: Saberes Necessários à Prática Educativa* [*Pedagogy of Freedom: Ethics, Democracy and Civic Courage*] (Freire, 1997/2000). Freire insisted on connecting our emotions with our reason. In Chapter 1 of this volume, Moacir Gadotti, a long-time colleague of Freire's, emphasizes this point. Freire, he recounts, spoke of a "reason soaked with emotion."

> He [Freire] was very insistent on this point. Education accounts for the creation of the freedom of every self-aware, perceptive, and responsible being, in which reason and emotion are in constant equilibrium and interaction. In the world of life the symbolic knowledge and the perceptive knowledge constantly interact. Knowledge is produced by human beings, beings of rationality and affection. Neither of these characteristics is superior to the other. It is always the subject who constructs categories of thought through her or his experiences with another person, in a given context, at a given moment. The affective aspect, in this construction, always remains. Omnipotent reason generates a bureaucratic and rationalist school, unable to understand the world of life and the human being in its entirety. It is a dogmatic and dormant school and not a living organism. We must understand the cognitive processes as vital processes insofar as the intellect and sensitivity are inseparable. (Gadotti, this volume)

Evaluation relevance today

> Persons are moved by emotion ... People are their emotions. To understand
> who a person is, it is necessary to understand emotion... . Emotions cut to
> the core of people. Within and through emotion people come to define the
> surface and essential, or core, meanings of who they are. Emotions and moods
> are ways of disclosing the world for the person. (Denzin, 2009, pp. 1–2)

When we engage with each other as whole human beings, both thinking and feeling come into play. We think about things and we care about
things. Ideally, we think about the things we care about and care about the
things we think about. Research in brain science, decision sciences, and
behavioral economics (Patton, 2014), to name but a few examples, has revealed the deep interconnections between thought and feeling, cognition
and emotion. Understanding and appreciating these interconnections are
manifest in approaches to evaluation that incorporate visualizations, videos,
art, and photography. Artistic and evocative approaches to evaluation want
to bring forth our emotional selves and do so by integrating art and science.
Science makes us think. Great art makes us feel. Great evaluations should
evoke both understandings (cognition) and feelings (emotions). Certainly
critical consciousness a la Freire has both cognitive and affection dimensions. His pedagogical insights provide inspiration about both why and how
to integrate thinking and feeling in a pedagogy of evaluation, teaching those
involved how to think evaluatively and acknowledge and express feelings
about the process and results.

Principle 7. Critical Consciousness Pedagogy Is Co-Intentional Education Among Those Involved in Whatever Roles

> A revolutionary leadership must accordingly practice *co-inten-tional* educa-
> tion. Teachers and students (leadership and people), co-intent on reality, are
> both Subjects, not only in the task of unveiling that reality, and thereby com-
> ing to know it critically, but in the task of re-creating that knowledge. As they
> attain this knowledge of reality through common reflection and action, they
> discover themselves as its permanent re-creators. In this way, the presence of
> the oppressed in the struggle for their liberation will be what it should be:
> not pseudo-participation, but committed involvement. (Freire, 1970, p. 69)

Evaluation relevance today. Developmental evaluation (DE), as one
example, is based on a *co-creation principle*: The innovation being evaluated and the evaluation develop together—interwoven, interdependent, iterative, and co-created – such that developmental evaluation becomes part
of the change process (Patton, 2015). This principle calls on developmental evaluators to acknowledge, document, report, and reflect on the ways
in which a developmental evaluation becomes part of the intervention. The

developmental evaluator gets close enough to the action to build a mutually trusting relationship with the social innovators. The quality of this collaboration derives in part from the capacity of the developmental evaluator to facilitate evaluative thinking, timely data-based feedback, and illuminative sense-making processes in support of innovation and adaptation. The developmental evaluator works *collaboratively* with social innovators to conceptualize, design, and test new approaches in an ongoing process of adaptation, intentional change, and *development*. DE is interactive—engaging social innovators, funders, supporters, and other core stakeholders to tailor and align the dynamics of innovation, development, adaptation, and evaluation. This dynamic amounts to the *co-creation* of both the unfolding innovation and the DE design (Lam & Shulha, 2015). The co-creation principle is a manifestation of a more general observation about collaborative processes of evaluation articulated by Cousins and Shulha (2006) in the *Handbook of Evaluation*: "Possibly the most significant development of the past decade in both research and evaluation communities has been a more general acceptance that *how* we work with clients and practitioners can be as meaningful and consequential as *what* we learn from our methods" (p. 277; emphasis in original).

The consequences of how evaluators work with participants in evaluation on the change process itself constitutes *process use* (Patton, 2008, 2012). Process use refers to the learning and behavior changes that occur among those involved in the evaluation from their involvement, for example, becoming more adept at evaluative questioning and thinking. Changes based on feedback of findings is *findings use*. Changes based on the processes of collaboration and co-creation constitute *process use*. For example, social innovators learning from a developmental evaluator how to articulate and use a complexity-based theory of change is process use. Participants in a social justice evaluation will learn how to analyze various inequities and injustices, and in that analysis the process of change has already been initiated.

Principle 8. Critical Consciousness Is Both Process and Outcome, Both Method and Result, Both Reflection and Action, Both Analytical and Change-Oriented

For Freire, the goal of critical consciousness as a pedagogy is "to be more fully human" (Freire, 1970, p. 55). He contrasts *being human* with the goal of having more wealth and possessions (p. 59). One doesn't attain critical consciousness as a fixed and defined outcome; rather it is an ever-emerging result of ongoing engagement and inquiry. He viewed critical pedagogy as both a method for making sense of the world and a new way of seeing and experiencing the world that yielded significant outcomes of new knowledge, new attitudes, new behaviors, and, ultimately, social change (p. 69). This is achieved through a process of sense-making that provides a new understanding of the world, which constitutes, as an outcome, a different kind of knowledge, which leads to social change.

> As a process of search, of knowledge, and thus of creation, it requires the investigators to discover the interpenetration of problems, in the linking of meaningful themes. The investigation will be most educational when it is most critical, and most critical when it avoids the narrow outlines of partial or "focalized" views of reality, and sticks to the comprehension of *total* reality. Thus, the process of searching for the meaningful thematics should include a concern for the links between themes, a concern to pose these themes as problems, and a concern for their historical–cultural context.
>
> Just as the educator may not elaborate a program to present *to* the people, neither may the investigator elaborate "itineraries" for researching the thematic universe, starting from points which *he* has predetermined. Both education and the investigation designed to support it must be "sympathetic" activities, in the etymological sense of the word. That is, they must consist of communication and of the common experience of a reality perceived in the complexity of its constant "becoming." (p. 108)

Evaluation relevance today. Those engaged in evaluation through the lens of critical analysis aim to make the inquiry a mechanism for bringing about social, cultural, economic, and political change. Eschewing any pretense of objectivity, they take an activist stance. Critical change inquiry aims to critique existing conditions and through that critique bring about change. Critical change evaluation criteria are derived from critical theory, which frames and engages in evaluation, from a Freirean perspective, with an explicit agenda of elucidating power, economic, and social inequalities.

The "critical" nature of critical theory flows from a commitment to go beyond just evaluating, but rather to use evaluation to critique society, raise consciousness, and change the balance of power in favor of those less powerful. Influenced by Marxism and Freirean pedagogy, informed by the presumption of the centrality of class conflict in understanding community and societal structures, and updated in the radical struggles of the 1960s, critical theory provides both philosophy and methods for approaching research and evaluation as fundamental and explicit manifestations of political praxis (connecting theory and action), and as change-oriented forms of engagement.

Critical social science and critical social theory attempt to understand, analyze, criticize, and alter social, economic, cultural, technological, and psychological structures and phenomena that have features of oppression, domination, exploitation, injustice, and misery. They do so with a view to changing or eliminating these structures and phenomena and expanding the scope of freedom, justice, and happiness. The assumption is that this knowledge will be used in processes of social change by people to whom understanding their situation is crucial in changing it (Bentz & Shapiro,

1998, p. 146; Kincheloe & McLaren, 2011). Critical change evaluation has three interconnected elements: (a) inquiry into situations of social injustice, (b) interpretation of the findings as a critique of the existing situation, and (c) using the findings and critique to mobilize and inform change. Critical theory looks at, exposes, and questions hegemony—traditional power assumptions held about relationships, groups, communities, societies, and organizations—to promote social change. Critical theory questions the assumed power that researchers typically hold over the people they typically research. Thus, critical change evaluation is based on the assumption that society is essentially discriminatory but is capable of becoming less so through purposeful human action. Critical evaluation also assumes that the dominant forms of professional research are discriminatory and must be challenged. Critical change evaluation takes the concept of knowledge as power and equalizes the generation of, access to, and use of that knowledge. Critical change evaluation is an ethical choice that gives voice to, and shares power with, previously marginalized and muted people (Davis, 2008, p. 140; Given, 2008, pp. 139–179; Schwandt, 2007, pp. 50–55). Feminist evaluation typically includes an explicit agenda of bringing about social change (e.g., Benmayor, 1991; Brisolara, Seigart, & SenGupta, 2104; Hesse-Biber, 2013; Podems, 2014). Liberation research and empowerment evaluation derive, in part, from Paulo Freire's philosophy of praxis and liberation education, articulated in his classics *Pedagogy of the Oppressed* (1970) and *Education for Critical Consciousness* (1973), still sources of influence and debate (e.g., Glass, 2001). Barone (2000) aspires to "emancipatory educational storysharing" (p. 247). Stephen Brookfield (2004) uses critical theory to illuminate adult education issues, trends, and inequities. Plummer (2011) integrates critical their and queer theory. Caruthers and Friend (2014) bring critical inquiry to online learning and engagement. Crave, Zaleski, and Trent (2014) emphasize the role of critical change in building a more equitable future through participatory program evaluation.

Here are examples offered by Davis (2008, p. 141). Martin Diskin worked with policy makers and development agencies in Latin American to conduct what they called "power structure research," in which they exposed injustice as a strategy for building coalitions and motivating movements. Christine Davis's evaluation of a children's mental health treatment team was conducted in partnership with community agencies and included examining issues of power, marginalization, and control within these teams. The results suggested rejection of the traditional hierarchical medical model of care and instead treating the patients as unique valuable humans and as equal partners in treatment (Davis, 2008, p. 141).

Principle 9. All Pedagogy Is Political

[L]earning between teachers and students is what gives educational practice its gnostic character. It is a practice that involves the use of methods, techniques, materials; in its directive character, it implies objectives, dreams, utopias, ideas. Hence we have the political nature of education and the capacity that all educational practices have in being political and never neutral. In being specifically human, education is gnostic and directive and for this reason, political. It is artistic and moral as it uses techniques as a means to facilitate teaching; it involves frustrations, fears, and desires. It requires of a teacher a general competence that involves knowledge of the nature of knowledge itself as well as the specific knowledges linked to one's field of specialization. (Freire, 2001, p. 67)

Evaluation relevance today

The social sciences ... should be used to improve quality of life ... for the oppressed, marginalized, stigmatized and ignored ... and to bring about healing, reconciliation and restoration between the researcher and the researched. (Stanfield, 2006, p. 725)

All inquiry is moral and political... . I want a discourse that troubles the world, understanding that inquiry can contribute to social justice. (Denzin, 2010, pp. 23–24)

A qualitative manifesto: A call to arms. Sociologist C. Wright Mills, a contemporary of Freire, also influenced by Marxism, wanted social science to make a difference in the lives of people. He challenged social scientists to help poor people take history into their own hands in order to "bend the structures of capitalism to the ideologies of radical democracy" (Denzin, 2010, pp. 23–24). Evaluation as a form of political activity can contribute to social justice in the following ways:

1. It can help identify different definitions of a problem and/or a situation that is being evaluated with some agreement that change is required. It can show, for example, how battered wives interpret the shelters, hotlines, and public services that are made available to them by social welfare agencies.
2. The assumptions, often belied by the facts of experience, that are held by various interested parties—policy makers, clients, welfare workers, online professionals—can be located and shown to be correct, or incorrect (Becker, 1967, p. 239).
3. Strategic points of intervention into social situations can be identified. Thus, the services of an agency and a program can be improved and evaluated.
4. It is possible to suggest "alternative moral points of view from which the problem, the policy and the program can be interpreted and assessed" (see Becker, 1967, pp. 239–240). Because of its emphasis on experience and its meanings, the interpretive method suggests that programs must always be judged by and from the point of view of the persons most directly affected (Denzin, 2010, pp. 24–25).

NEW DIRECTIONS FOR EVALUATION • DOI: 10.1002/ev

Principle 10. Critical Pedagogy Is Fundamentally and Continuously Evaluative

Critical consciousness involves ongoing evaluation. The development of a literacy campaign scenario presented earlier, which is the most extended example of Freire's approach in *Pedagogy of the Oppressed,* describes in depth and detail a participatory evaluation process. But critical pedagogy is not conceptualized as a project, and the purpose is not to produce a report. Critical pedagogy is an ongoing process that aims to bring about long-term and lasting change.

Triangulation

I derived these 10 pedagogical principles from Freire's writings. I did so without reading any of the chapters in this volume written by Brazilians who are Freirean experts and his colleagues. Having independently identified the principles, I examined the two chapters in Part 1 to find out if the principles were manifest and evident in those writings. Indeed, they were. Table 3.1 summarizes and gives examples of this triangulation.

Beyond the triangulation of principles in Table 3.1, Chapters 4 and 5 explicitly address and assess the Freirean pedagogical principles identified and explicated in this chapter.

Evaluation Relevance Today: Freire's Pedagogical Principles Connected to Evaluation Approaches

Table 3.2 summarizes some prominent and important developments in evaluation as they connect and relate to, and have been influenced by, Freire's principles.

A Holistic Freirean Evaluation Framework

Freire was philosophically grounded in Hegelian dialectics. What most strikes me about his pedagogy is his genius for synthesis. His capacity to transcend thesis and antithesis to generate integrated synthesis undergirds all 10 principles identified and discussed in this chapter. He emphasized throughout *Pedagogy of the Oppressed* that both the oppressors and the oppressed must achieve critical consciousness and do so for the advancement of each and both together (Principle 1). He connected the individual to community (Principle 2) and people to each other (Principle 3). He integrated reflection and action (Principle 4), objectivity and subjectivity (Principle 5), thinking and emotion (Principle 6), and evaluators and participants in evaluation (Principle 7). He emphasized the interconnection and interrelationship between process and outcome, methods and results, analysis and engagement, and understanding and social change (Principle 8).

Table 3.1. Triangulation of Perspectives. Supporting Evidence for and Interpretation of Freirean Pedagogical Principles from Brazilian Chapters 1 and 2

Freirean Pedagogical Principle	Chapter 1, Gadotti	Chapter 2, Firme and Stone
1. Use evaluative thinking to open up, develop, and nurture *critical consciousness*.	Emancipatory pedagogies, like the pedagogy of the oppressed, propose methods in which the teaching–learning process involve evaluation as part of developing critical thinking.	The intent is to highlight the validity of Freire's ideas for evaluative thinking in the context of street education. An overall *critical* structural approach, in tune with Freire's ideas and concerns, emerged to overcome the perverse cycle of institutionalization, deportation and imprisonment, and to promote and defend the human rights and citizenship of the children.
2. Consciousness resides in communities of people, not just individuals.	Pedagogical action through interdisciplinarity calls for building participatory learning communities.	Purpose: To promote shared learning from community experience and use collective knowledge to work more effectively with street children.
3. Critical consciousness pedagogy must be interactive and dialogical.	The principles and premises of popular education are the foundations of collaborative dialogical evaluation—an evaluation done *with* those who are learning, not *to* them,	Collectively, the programs were multidimensional in intent and methods. And their educational methods always preserved the liberty of the children, leaving them free to make all their own decisions. Dialogue and critical thinking marked the methods.
4. Integrate reflection and action.	Transforming praxis, grounded in reflection, leads to social and communicative action, and productive work.	The evaluation reflections and conclusions were *experientially-arrived-at*, based on participation and knowledge exchange in the context.
5. Value and integrate the objective and subjective.	Being and knowing are inextricably linked. Knowledge is a social construction.	The intent was to infuse enlightened subjectivity into the evaluative process in accordance with the Freirean principle of valuing and integrating the objective and subjective ... The evaluators learned to

(Continued)

NEW DIRECTIONS FOR EVALUATION • DOI: 10.1002/ev

Table 3.1. Continued

Freirean Pedagogical Principle	Chapter 1, Gadotti	Chapter 2, Firme and Stone
		face the challenge of making human subjectivity an asset rather than a liability, by combining critical thinking with creativity for making enlightened choices.
6. Integrate thinking and emotion.	Lesson 1: Reason and emotion are interconnected.	For the evaluators, learning to be *human instruments* was crucial, which in the study context, meant practice of Freirean principles. Fundamentally it meant openness. On one level it required a certain "value reorientation" to be able to practice empathy and sensitivity in interactions with people. Curiously, this implied being nonjudgmental, which the evaluators found to be a parallel to the *neutral* posture in the scientific sense—however it meant to be "close and caring," not "cold and distant."
7. Critical consciousness pedagogy is co-intentional education among those involved in whatever roles.	Lesson 3: There is no teaching without learning, and no learning without teaching. Critical pedagogy is dialogic.	Freire maintained that *one cannot teach without learning, nor learn without teaching.* The two acts are simultaneous, and there is knowledge exchange.
8. Critical consciousness is both process and outcome, both method and result, and both analytical and change-oriented.	Lesson 4: Pedagogy involves both being and knowing. To educate is to read the world in order to be able to transform it. Paulo Freire was a man of praxis, both a thinker and a doer.	Freirean openness meant critical thinking. The evaluators learned to question their methodological choices every step of the way, devising context-appropriate methods and measures without compromising data quality, but in fact enhancing it through creativity ... Emergent from the

(Continued)

Table 3.1. Continued

Freirean Pedagogical Principle	Chapter 1, Gadotti	Chapter 2, Firme and Stone
		naturalistic–responsive evaluation process was also a methodology for collecting and compiling authentic and credible data for continuous program monitoring and improvement.
9. All pedagogy is political.	Freirean pedagogy is essentially about the construction of a fair, democratic society. All education and all evaluation presuppose a societal project, which makes both inherently political.	The needs of street children is not only a question of economic development but also very much a question of political will. Basing evaluation on Freirean pedagogy using naturalistic–responsive methods is both feasible and effective in an emotionally and politically sensitive context.
10. Critical pedagogy is fundamentally evaluative.	For Paulo Freire, the question of method is crucial in the educational act, as it is in the evaluative act: When we use a certain method, which is not neutral, we do it based on an ethical political and pedagogical choice. See also Gadotti (1994).	What did the evaluators teach? What knowledge did they impart? Perhaps the most valuable teaching, especially on the level of the program staff, as well as street children, was the knowledge that evaluation is a friend, not a foe; that evaluators can be trusted as human beings, and as professionals; that data serve a common cause, and not always used for individual exploitation.

He portrayed cultural patterns, social interactions, community relationships, economic dynamics, socio-psychological manifestations, knowledge, education, and learning manifestations as fundamentally political; he made sense of everything through the lens of political economy, and showed the oppressed how to understand their situations historically and currently through that lens; thus did he connect the past to the present and future pedagogically and paradigmatically (Principle 9). Finally, he brought what today we call evaluative thinking into his analysis, engagement process, and sense-making, facilitating the oppressed, nonliterate,

Table 3.2. Freire's Pedagogical Principles Connected to Evaluation Approaches

Freire's Pedagogical Principles	Resonant Evaluation Approaches
1. Use evaluative thinking to open up, develop, and nurture *critical consciousness*.	1. *Critical consciousness* is the foundation of evaluation undertaken from a social justice perspective (House, 1976, 1990, 2014, 2015; Kirkhart, 1994; Ryan & DeStefano, 2000). Methodologically, it includes attention to reflexivity and praxis (Patton, 2015). Evaluative thinking (in contrast to conducting evaluations) has emerged as an important result of stakeholder involvement in evaluation (Carden & Earl, 2007; Patton, 2008, 2012).
2. Consciousness resides in communities of people, not just individuals.	2. Community as a reservoir of knowledge is the foundation of participatory, collaborative, and empowerment evaluation (Cousins & Chouinard, 2012; Cousins & Earl, 1992, 1995; Cousins, Whitmore, & Shulha, 2014; Fetterman, Rodríguez-Campos, Wandersman, & O'Sullivan, 2014; Fetterman & Wandersman, 2005).
3. Critical consciousness pedagogy must be interactive and dialogical.	3. Democratic dialogic evaluation integrates social justice with interactive and dialogical processes (House & Howe, 2000).
4. Integrate reflection and action.	4. Reflective practice as a core evaluation practitioner competency (King & Podems, 2014; King & Stevahn, 2013; King, Stevahn, Ghere, & Minnema, 2001; Schon, 1983, 1987). Reflective practice includes attention to reflexivity and praxis (Patton, 2015).
5. Value and integrate the objective and subjective.	5. Responsive evaluation (Guba & Lincoln, 1981; Stake, 1975, 1978, 1996) and mixed methods (Greene, 2007).
6. Integrate thinking and emotion.	6. Evocative evaluation; multivocal evaluation (Patton, 2015).
7. Critical consciousness pedagogy is co-intentional education among those involved in whatever roles.	7. Co-evolution (Patton, 2011) and feminist evaluation (Podems, 2010, 2013).
8. Critical consciousness is both process and outcome, both method and result, and both analytical and change-oriented.	8. Developmental evaluation (Patton, 2011, 2015) and process use (Cousins, 2008; Patton, 2008, 2012).
9. All pedagogy is political.	9. All evaluation is political (House, 1973; Patton, 2008, 2012; Weiss, 1993).
10. Critical pedagogy is fundamentally evaluative.	10. Evaluative thinking embedded in evaluation processes and methods (Patton, 2008, 2012).

NEW DIRECTIONS FOR EVALUATION • DOI: 10.1002/ev

poor, and disadvantaged to describe, compare, analyze, reflect, and render judgments as the basis for bringing about change.

Pedagogy of Evaluation

There is no singular or monolithic pedagogy of evaluation. As I said in opening this chapter, embedded in different evaluation approaches are varying assumptions, values, premises, priorities, sense-making processes, and principles. Thus, those who participate in an evaluation are experiencing sometimes explicit, more often implicit and tacit, pedagogical principles. Evaluation invites those involved to see the world in a certain way, to make sense of it through a particular lens, to make judgments based on certain kinds of evidence and values. Those evaluation approaches that have been most influenced by Freirean pedagogy and share Freirean values, modes of engagement, and desired outcomes are social-justice–focused evaluations, democratic deliberative evaluation, empowerment evaluation, feminist evaluation, transformative evaluation, and critical systems evaluation. Other evaluation approaches value, teach, and strive for different results; that is, they are based on other pedagogical premises and principles.

The larger understanding that Freire's work reminds us of is that all evaluation approaches constitute a pedagogy of some kind. All evaluation teaches something. What is taught and how it is taught varies, but evaluation is inherently and predominantly a pedagogical interaction. Freire understood and taught us that all interactions between and among people are pedagogical, something is always being taught, conveyed, and proselytized. What is your pedagogy of evaluation?

References

Agar, M. (2013). *The lively science: Remodeling human social research.* Minneapolis, MN: Mill City Press.
Arendt, H.. (1968). *Between past and future: Eight exercises in political thought.* New York: Viking.
Barone, T. (2000). *Aesthetics, politics, and educational inquiry: Essays and examples.* New York, NY: Peter Lang.
Becker, H. S. (1967). Whose side are we on? *Social Problems, 14*(3), n 239–247.
Benmayor, R. (1991). Testimony, action research, and empowerment: Puerto Rican women and popular education. In S. B. Gluck & D. Patai (Eds.), *Women's words: The feminist practice of oral history* (pp. 159–174). New York, NY: Routledge.
Bentz, V. M., & Shapiro, J. J. (1998). *Mindful inquiry in social research.* London: Sage Publications.
Better Evaluation. (2014). *Collaborative outcomes reporting.* Retrieved from http://betterevaluation.org/plan/approach/cort
Brisolara, S., Seigart, D., & SenGupta, S. (Eds.). (2014). *Feminist evaluation and research: Theory and practice.* New York, NY: Guilford Press.
Brookfield, S. D. (2004). Critical thinking techniques. In M. G. Galbraith (Ed.), *Adult learning methods: A guide for effective instruction* (3rd ed.; pp. 341–360). Malabar, FL: Krieger.

Carden, F., & Earl, S. (2007). Infusing evaluative thinking as process use: The case of the International Development Research Centre (IDRC). *New Directions for Evaluation, 116*, 61–73.

Caruthers, L., & Friend, J. (2014). Critical pedagogy in online environments as thirdspace: A narrative analysis of voices of candidates in educational preparatory programs. *Educational Studies, 50*(1), 8–35.

Cousins, J. B. (Ed.). (2008). *Process use in theory, research, and practice. New Directions for Evaluation, 116.*

Cousins, J. B., & Chouinard, J. A. (2012). *Participatory evaluation up close: An integration of research-based knowledge.* Charlotte, NC: Information Age.

Cousins, J. B., & Earl, L. M. (1992). The case for participatory evaluation. *Educational Evaluation and Policy Analysis, 14*(4), 397–418.

Cousins, J. B., & Earl, L. M. (1995). *Participatory evaluation in education: Studies in evaluation use and organizational learning.* London, England: Falmer Press.

Cousins, J. B. & Shulha, L.M. (2006). A comparative analysis of evaluation utilization and its cognate fields of inquiry: current issues and trends." PP. 266–291 in I. F. Shaw, J. C. Greene, & M. M. Mark (Eds.), *The Sage handbook of evaluation: policies, programs and practices.* Thousand Oaks, CA: Sage.

Cousins, J. B., Whitmore, E., & Shulha, L. (2014). Let there be light. *American Journal of Evaluation, 35*(1), 149–153.

Crave, M., Zaleski, K., & Trent, T. (2014). *Do your participatory methods contribute to an equitable future?* Retrieved from http://aea365.org/blog/pd-presenters-week-mary-crave-kerry-zaleski-and-tererai-trenton-do-your-participatory-methods-contribute-to-an-equitablefuture/?utm_source=feedburner&utm_medium=email&utm_campaign=Feed%3A+aea365+%28AEA365%29

Davis, C. S. (2008). Critical action research. In L. M. Given (Ed.), *The SAGE encyclopedia of qualitative research methods* (Vol. 1, pp. 139–142). Thousand Oaks, CA: Sage.

Denzin, N. K. (2009). *On understanding emotion.* New Brunswick, NJ: Transaction.

Denzin, N. K. (2010). *The qualitative manifesto: A call to arms.* Walnut Creek, CA: Left Coast Press.

Fetterman, D. M., Rodríguez-Campos, L., Wandersman, A., & O'Sullivan, R. G. (2014). Collaborative, participatory, and empowerment evaluation: Building a strong conceptual foundation for stakeholder involvement approaches to evaluation. *American Journal of Evaluation, 35*(1), 144–148.

Fetterman, D. M., & Wandersman, A. (2005). *Empowerment evaluation principles and practice.* New York, NY: Guilford Press.

Freire, P. (1970/2000). *Pedagogy of the oppressed* (Bloomsbury paperback edition). New York, NY: Bloomsbury.

Freire, P. (1973). *Education for critical consciousness.* New York: Bloomsbury Publishing.

Freire, P. (1997/2001). *Pedagogy of the freedom: Ethics, democracy, and civic courage.* Lantham, MD: Rowman & Littlefield.

Gadotti, M. (1994). *Reading Paulo Freire. His life and work.* Albany, NY: State University of New York Press.

Given, L. M. (Ed.). (2008). *The SAGE encyclopedia of qualitative research methods.* Thousand Oaks, CA: Sage.

Glass, R. (2001). On Paulo Freire's philosophy of praxis and themfoundations of liberation education. *Educational Researcher, 30*(2), 15–25.

Greene, J. C. (2007). *Mixed methods in social inquiry.* San Francisco, CA: Jossey-Bass

Guba, E. G., & Lincoln, Y. S. (1981). *Effective evaluation: Improving the usefulness of evaluation results through responsive and naturalistic approaches.* San Francisco, CA: Jossey-Bass.

House, E. R. (1973). *School evaluation: The politics and process.* New York, NY: McCutchan.

House, E. R. (1976). Justice in evaluation. *Evaluation Studies Review Annual, 1,* 75–100.

House, E. R. (1977). *The logic of evaluative argument.* Los Angeles, CA: Center for the Study of Evaluation.

House, E. R. (1990). Methodology and justice. *New Directions for Evaluation, 45,* 23–36.

House, E. R. (2014). *Evaluating: Values, biases, and practical wisdom.* Charlotte, NC: Information Age.

House, E. R. (2015, November 13). *Social justice, racism, and culturally responsive evaluation.* Plenary presentation at the Annual Meeting of the American Evaluation Association, Chicago, IL.

House, E. R., & Howe, K. (2000). Deliberative democratic evaluation. *New Directions for Evaluation, 85,* 3–12.

Kincheloe, J. L., & McLaren, P. (2011). Rethinking critical theory and qualitative research. In J. L. Kincheloe, K. Hayes, S. R. Steinberg, & K. G. Tobin (Eds.), *Key works in critical pedagogy.* Rotterdam, The Netherlands: Sense Publishers.

King, J. A., & Podems, D. (Eds.). (2014). Professionalizing evaluation: A global perspective on evaluator competencies [Special issue]. *Canadian Journal of Program Evaluation, 28*(3).

King, J. A., & Stevahn, L. (2013). *Interactive evaluation practice: Mastering the interpersonal dynamics of program evaluation.* Thousand Oaks, CA: Sage.

King, J. A., Stevahn, L., Ghere, G., & Minnema, J. (2001). Toward a taxonomy of essential evaluator competencies. *American Journal of Evaluation, 22*(2), 229–247.

Kirkhart, K. (1994). *Presidential address on evaluation and social justice.* Annual Meeting of the American Evaluation Association, Boston, MA.

Kushner, S. (2000). *Personalizing evaluation.* London: Sage.

Kushner, S. (2016). *Evaluative research methods: Managing the complexities of judgment in the field.* New York: IAP.

Lam, C. Y., & Shulha, L. M. (2015). Insights on using developmental evaluation for innovating: A case study on the cocreation of an innovative program. *American Journal of Evaluation, 36*(3), 358–374.

Mansuri, G., & Vijayendra, R. (2012). *Localizing development: Does participation work?* Washington, DC: World Bank.

MacDonald, B. (1987). Evaluation and the control of education. In R. Murphy & H. Torrance (Eds.), *Issues and methods in evaluation* (pp. 36–48). London: Paul Chapman.

Mertens, D. M. (1998). *Research methods in education and psychology: Integrating diversity with quantitative and qualitative approaches.* Thousand Oaks, CA: Sage.

Mertens, D. M. (1999). Inclusive evaluation: Implications of transformative theory for evaluation. *American Journal of Evaluation, 20*(1), 1–14.

Patton, M. Q. (2008). *Utilization-focused evaluation.* Thousand Oaks, CA: Sage.

Patton, M. Q. (2011). *Developmental evaluation: Applying complexity concepts to enhance innovation and use.* New York, NY: Guilford Press.

Patton, M. Q. (2012). *Essentials of utilization-focused evaluation.* Thousand Oaks, CA: Sage.

Patton, M. Q. (2014). What brain sciences reveal about integrating theory and practice. *American Journal of Evaluation, 35*(2), 237–244.

Patton, M. Q. (2015). The developmental evaluation mindset: Eight guiding principles. In M. Q. Patton, K. McKegg, & N. Wehipeihana (Eds.), *Developmental evaluation exemplars: Principles in practice* (Chapter 15). New York, NY: Guilford.

Patton, M. Q. (2017). *Principles-focused evaluation.* New York, NY: Guilford.

Pietro, D. S. (1983). *Evaluation sourcebook for private and voluntary organizations.* New York, NY: American Council of Voluntary Agencies for Foreign Service.

Plummer, K. (2011). Critical humanism and queer theory. In N. K. Denzin & Y. S. Lincoln (Eds.), *The SAGE handbook of qualitative research* (4th ed., pp. 195–207). Thousand Oaks, CA: Sage.

Podems, D. (2010). Feminist evaluation and gender approaches: There's a difference. *Journal of MultiDisciplinary Evaluation*, 6(14). Retrieved from file:///C:/Documents%20and%20Settings/quads/My%20Documents/199-943-1-PB.pdf

Podems, D. (2013, September 17). Feminist evaluation for non-feminist evaluators (AEA365 blog post). Retrieved from http://aea365.org/blog/fiemme-week-donna-podems-on-applying-feminist-evaluation-for-non-feminist-evaluators/

Podems, D. (2014). Feminist evaluation for nonfeminists. In S. Brisolara, D. Seigart, & S. SenGupta (Eds.), *Feminist evaluation and research: Theory and practice* (Chap. 5, pp. 113–142). New York, NY: Guilford Press.

Private Agencies Collaborating Together. (1986). *Participatory evaluation*. New York, NY: Author.

Ryan, K. E., & DeStefano, L. (Eds.). (2000). *Evaluation as a democratic process: promoting inclusion, dialogue, and deliberation*. New Directions for Evaluation, 85.

Salmen, L. F., & Kane, E. (2006). *Bridging diversity: Participatory learning for responsive development*. Washington, DC: World Bank

Schon, D. A. (1983). *The reflective practitioner: How professionals think in action*. New York, NY: Basic Books.

Schon, D. A. (1987). *Educating the reflective practitioner: Toward a new design for teaching and learning in the professions*. San Francisco, CA: Jossey-Bass.

Schwandt, T. A. (2007). *The SAGE dictionary of qualitative inquiry* (3rd ed.). Thousand Oaks, CA: Sage.

Schwandt, T. (2015). Reconstructing professional ethics and responsibility: Implications of critical systems thinking. *Evaluation*, 21(4), 462–466.

Scriven, M. (2015). Evaluation revolution. *Journal of MultiDisciplinary Evaluation*, 11(25), 14–21.

Stake, R. E. (1975). *Evaluating the arts in education: A responsive approach*. Columbus, OH: Charles E. Merrill.

Stake, R. E. (1978). The case study method in a social inquiry. *Educational Researcher*, 7, 5–8.

Stake, R. E. (1995). *The art of case study research*. Thousand Oaks, CA: Sage.

Stake, R. E. (2004). How far dare an evaluator go toward saving themworld? Beyond neutrality: What evaluators care about. *American Journal of Evaluation*, 25(1), 103–107.

Stanfield, J. H., II. (2006). The possible restorative justice functions of qualitative research. *International Journal of Qualitative Studies in Education*, 19(6), 723–727.

Weiss, C. H. (1993). Where politics and evaluation research meet. *American Journal of Evaluation*, 14(1), 93–106.

MICHAEL QUINN PATTON, *founder and director of Utilization-Focused Evaluation, has over 45 years of experience as an independent evaluation consultant and is the author of several evaluation books including* Developmental Evaluation: Applying Complexity Concepts to Enhance Innovation and Use *and* Principles-Focused Evaluation.

Chianca, T. K., Ceccon, C. (2017). Pedagogy in process applied to evaluation: Learning from paulo freire's work in Guinea-Bissau. In M. Q. Patton (Ed.), *Pedagogy of Evaluation. New Directions for Evaluation*, 155, 79–97.

4

Pedagogy in Process Applied to Evaluation: Learning from Paulo Freire's Work in Guinea-Bissau

Thomaz K. Chianca, Claudius Ceccon

Abstract

This chapter presents and discusses a practical case where Paulo Freire and a group of his close Brazilian colleagues applied, created, adapted or re-created some of his main philosophical ideas on pedagogy to educational reform in Guinea-Bissau, West Africa, shortly after that country's independence from Portugal. Their challenge was to help the country face a huge level of illiteracy among the Guineans. After describing what was developed, the authors assess the extent to which the 10 principles introduced in Chapter 3 of this volume are manifest in the Guinea-Bissau experience. They find that 8 of the 10 principles were clearly operational and add two additional Freirean principles that characterized the work in Guinea-Bissau. The implications for evaluation pedagogy are discussed and illustrated. © 2017 Wiley Periodicals, Inc., and the American Evaluation Association.

Paulo Freire and the Guinea-Bissau Context

P aulo Freire, Brazilian educator, deeply believed that people are the subject of their own learning. One of his main conceptions is that educators and educatees learn together, in a dynamic relationship in which practice, intermingled with theory, reinvents itself as part of a continuous process of improvement. According to Freire, educators must not use education as a way to conform people to current norms. If their practice is coherent to the idea that to educate means to free/empower people, then they have to be facilitators of the learning process and understand that they are engaged in a two-way road, where they learn while teaching.

This implies that educators should not work with preconceived schemes/plans. Rather, they should engage in a dialectic process with the people, who will provide the elements on which to build together the best approaches and strategies for their specific context, culture, and demands. He defends the need for a deep, revolutionary, dialogical commitment between educators and educatees for any educational process to be successful.

This chapter will present and discuss a practical case where Paulo Freire and a group of his close Brazilian colleagues applied, created, adapted, or re-created some of his main philosophical ideas on pedagogy. The case refers to the opportunity Freire and his colleagues had in the mid-1970s to work with the government of a, at the time, recently independent country in West Africa—Guinea-Bissau. Their challenge was to help the country address a huge level of illiteracy among the Guineans. The initial invitation was to develop a national literacy program soon after that country had gained its independence from Portugal in the early 1970s, after a guerrilla war that started in the late 1950s. We will tell the story through the eyes of one of the authors of this paper (Claudius Ceccon) who was one of Paulo Freire's colleagues working with him throughout this project (1975–1980) and participated in all site visits to that country.

Pedagogy in Process was how Freire titled the English version of his book on their experience in Guinea-Bissau (Freire, 1978). The title expresses closely what they did: (a) a constant effort for an in-depth immersion in the country's history, culture, and current reality; (b) the establishment of strong and dialectical connections with key stakeholders; and (c) the permanent creation and reinvention of a literacy program that was being always adapted and improved without losing its connection with the main ideal of contributing for the country's efforts of reconstruction. Freire's ideas expressed on this experience on the need for programs/pedagogies to adapt constantly in the face of complex realities and to focus on being relevant to a social cause seem clearly connected and have probably inspired many prominent evaluation approaches we know today, such as developmental evaluation (Patton, 2011), empowerment evaluation (Fetterman, 2001), responsive evaluation (Stake, 2004), and deliberative democratic evaluation (House & Howe, 1999).

As we describe and reflect upon this rich experience in Guinea-Bissau, with some first-hand information, we will identify instances where some of the 10 pedagogical principles Patton extracted from Freire's writings (see Chapter 3 of this volume) are evident. Also, a couple of other principles, with relevance to evaluation theory and practice, will be introduced as part of a critical analysis of Freire's experience in that country.

NEW DIRECTIONS FOR EVALUATION • DOI: 10.1002/ev

The Guinea-Bissau Project

Freire, a schoolteacher living in the city of Recife, capital of Pernambuco State, in the early 1960s proved that illiterate peasants could learn to read and write in 40 hours (Pelandré, 2002). As part of the same process, they could also learn to develop critical thinking—what Freire called "conscientization" (Freire Institute, n.d.). Freire's educational method helped people understand the determinants of their unjust reality and to reflect about actions they should take to change it. In recognition of his successful work, Freire was invited by the Ministry of Education to organize a National Literacy Program, from the nation's capital Brasilia (Brazil, 1964).

Unfortunately, his work was cut short after a military–civilian coup in 1964 started 21 years of a military dictatorship in Brazil. Freire, accused of subversion, was arrested and thrown in prison. After his release, he had to go into exile, first to Bolivia and then to Chile, where he worked at the Institute of Agrarian Reform, during all Eduardo Frei's presidency (1964–1970). In 1970, he was invited by the World Council of Churches, based in Geneva, Switzerland, to be the head of its educational division.

In Geneva, Freire and three Brazilian colleagues (Miguel Darcy de Oliveira, Rosiska Darcy de Oliveira, and Claudius Ceccon) created the Institute of Cultural Action—Idac (French acronym). They wanted to contribute to a better world through education by developing and disseminating critical reflections about Freire's experience in designing the Brazilian National Literacy Program and in implementing conscientization programs with Chilean peasants. Their work started to attract attention from European groups frustrated with the authoritarianism of their societies, which was reflected in the teacher/student relations, or doctors/patients, trade unionist leaders/workers, politicians/voters and so on. The idea was to bring to those groups a new political–pedagogical proposal based on the principle that every educative action must produce new knowledge.

It was at that point, in the spring of 1975, that the Idac office received a letter from Mario Cabral, Minister of Education for the newly born Republic of Guinea-Bissau (West Africa), inviting Paulo Freire and the Idac team to conduct a national adult literacy campaign.

Idac First Encounter With Guinea-Bissau

There was the excitement of the challenge and the curiosity to know the country whose struggle, led by a mythical leader, Amilcar Cabral, succeeded to defeat the powerful and well-equipped Portuguese colonial army. At the same time, Idac knew the expectations were high, and the challenge was humongous. After many discussions they responded that they needed to know the situation and real needs better, before they could consider a formal collaboration. With the World Council of Churches' support, the Idac team was able to visit Guinea-Bissau a few months after receiving the invitation from Mario Cabral.

NEW DIRECTIONS FOR EVALUATION • DOI: 10.1002/ev

For Brazilians living in exile in a European country for years—which seemed an eternity—the Idac team found that Guinea-Bissau had familiar characteristics, as immediately identified upon their arrival. There were the green mango trees, seeming to shine under the hot sun; the cordiality, the warmness of the people; their way of smiling, touching, embracing, and walking at a nonchalant rhythm that made them somehow nostalgic of Brazil. The Guineans' Portuguese accent and the team's Brazilian accent didn't hinder communication. They even succeeded to incorporate a few terms in creole, the *lingua franca* that bridged the dialects of some 40 ethnic Guinean groups. However, it took them some time to understand that behind many common behaviors and characteristics there were also, as one would expect, important cultural differences.

During this first visit, the Idac team met with several key stakeholders—from the President himself and his ministers to peasants in the countryside and urban areas in the periphery of Bissau; from military responsible for maintaining the political line set by Amilcar Cabral to the "Homens Grandes"—the Elders, respected wise men that keep the tradition, the culture, and the history of the people. The team met with teachers and government officials, especially the team of the Ministry of Education responsible for the creation of the new school system for the whole country. They also collected as many relevant documents as they could find, took extensive notes and pictures, and discussed at length with the team from the Ministry of Education about strategic issues concerning adult education. The Idac team was trying to build a common understanding of the task at hand, so that they could consider, with greater clarity, whether they would eventually be able to help.

It was the rainy season and there were no roads that could take the Idac team to places far away from the capital Bissau, so they had to fly in huge military helicopters. Their Russian pilots, with a hand-made map on their knees, oriented themselves following, at low altitudes and at eye sight, the meanders of the rivers below. On one of the trips, the helicopter landed to disembark some passengers. The Idac team disembarked with them, to discover, just after the helicopter took off, that they had been left in the wrong village. No radio to call it back. It rained heavily and continuously.

The main authority of that village (called "Governor") was warned that Paulo Freire was at the "airport"—an open wooded structure covered with palm tree leaves. Paulo Freire and Elza, his wife, were hosted by the village's Governor at one of the few houses left intact by the Portuguese. The rest of the team was distributed among several semidestroyed houses. Comfort was at a minimum for the foreigners—toilet basins broken, no electricity, high temperatures and humidity, and bugs everywhere. The Governor shared the little food he had. There was, however, plenty of time to talk with the local people and educators before they were rescued 24 hours later. That nonprogrammed visit was a realistic counterpoint to the one the Idac team had with Julio de Andrade, the military responsible for the Party's line, some days before. He presented the general political orientation to Guinea-Bissau. The local villagers and educators spoke of their concrete conditions. After these and many other encounters, the Idac team left the country, realizing the huge challenge the Guineans (and them) had to face.

Approaching the Work in Guinea-Bissau

Back to Geneva, the team went through all the evidence they had gathered. It was a very rich exercise of mounting a puzzle with each one's particular views and experiences. It showed how different were the perceptions and values for each team member. Out of the innumerable discussions emerged clearly the main question that the Guineans had to address: *What kind of educational system should they build?*

In reality, there were two very different educational systems in place at that moment. The first was the one brought by the Portuguese, which was essentially a poor transposition of the metropolis model: a caricature, a selective school, in line with the colonialists' interests. It existed practically only in Bissau. The teachers used Portuguese, a language spoken by no more than 5% of the population. The curriculum was Portugal's geography, hydrography, railroad network, and history. In those books, Africa didn't exist before the arrival of the conquerors. "In every rainy season the river besides the school flooded the whole village. We knew the names of all the rivers in Portugal, but didn't know this one," told a teacher to the Idac team. That school system had no other purpose than to de-Africanize and alienate the students from their national reality. At the end of this very selective process, a few students went to Portugal to finish their education at the University of Coimbra. They were told of their superiority over their fellow citizens. Their mission was to impose and maintain colonial rule in the Portuguese-dominated territories of Angola, Moçambique, São Tomé e Príncipe, Cape Verde, and Guinea-Bissau. That's what that education was meant for.

The other system sprouted from the schools that were organized in the liberated areas, during the struggle for independence. There, the process of learning necessarily happened in close relation with practice, because everybody had to do what was necessary for survival. It started by learning to dig trenches to protect themselves from air raids and plant what was necessary to eat. In that system, the elders, the repository of culture and history, played an important role. However, at the same time, it was paramount to overcome certain myths of the cultural heritage—either because they contradicted the pursuit of new times, or because science could better explain natural phenomena than the wrath of gods. The place of women in the new society was also one of the main concerns and important changes needed to happen on this front, too.

These two educational systems were in opposition. After extensive discussions between the Idac team and the Ministry of Education adult edu-

NEW DIRECTIONS FOR EVALUATION • DOI: 10.1002/ev

cation team, it became clear that the best choice was to invest in improving the system created during the struggle for independence. There were serious obstacles, though: not enough trained teachers, no new curriculum developed, no adequate books or other educational materials. Therefore, it was not possible to implement a completely new system instantly. A period of transition, as short as possible, was necessary. The new system would have to be steadily created and reinforced in coexistence with the old. Changes would efface the most negative characteristics of the old system, until conditions were ripe to implement the "new school" fully.

In constant communication with Idac, the Ministry of Education decided to adopt, as part of their educational approach to the whole system, Freire's ideas on connecting education to action as a way to understand reality and address real-life needs and situations. Schools should promote a total educational process, as an end in itself and not just to fulfill a requirement for children to advance to higher grades. The objective of education should be to help improve the communities' reality. To implement those changes, it would be necessary to undertake a series of structural changes including the creation of an Adult Education Department and Integrated Popular Education Centers (CEPIs).

Freire's Core Strategies

Freire's education and action approach had basically three strategies:

1. Critically understand reality through the establishment of an in-depth dialogue with the local people taking into account their accumulated knowledge and culture rooted in traditions, so that they could realize both their potentials and limitations.
2. Conduct scientific studies to bridge knowledge gaps, to clarify some key aspects and to look for generator themes.
3. Application of the new knowledge in practical projects to address the most important issues within the communities, especially the ones related to improving production.

There were some successes in the process, some failures, and some mixed results. But after 5 years and a military coup, the team decided that the challenges were too great, and the initiative ended. The purpose of the remainder of this chapter is to examine the extent to which the 10 pedagogical principles Patton extracted from Freire's writings (Chapter 3 of this volume) are evident in the Guinea-Bissau experience.

The 10 Pedagogical Principles and the Guinea-Bissau Experience

The work of Freire and his colleagues in Guinea-Bissau, without question, was one of the most relevant examples of applying Freire's theories and praxis on education and literacy. Given the richness of the experience, we

will discuss pedagogical principles relevant to evaluation theory and practice that can be drawn from a critical analysis of the Guinea-Bissau project.

Our analysis found explicit evidence of all but 2 of the 10 pedagogical
principles identified by Patton. The missing ones were 5 (value and integrate the objective and subjective) and 6 (integrate thinking and emotion).
The following is a reflective account of the evidence found for each pedagogical principle. Unless otherwise noted, all quotations from now on are
taken from Freire's book *Pedagogy in Process: The Letters to Guinea-Bissau*
(Freire, 1978).

**Freire's Pedagogical Principle 1: Use Evaluative Thinking to Open Up,
Develop, and Nurture Critical Consciousness**

This principle was clearly embedded in all activities proposed by Idac's
team in their work with the Ministry of Education in Guinea-Bissau. Freire
constantly stresses that his approach aims at conscientization of people or
the awakening of people's critical consciousness or critical thinking, what
Scriven (1994) would also call evaluative thinking—being thoughtful or
analytic about whatever is being evaluated. This key aspect becomes apparent when Freire explains how the learning process between educators and
educatees should be based on a critical attitude about the aspects that will
serve to mediate their mutual learning.

> Rather, in the connection between the educator and the learner, mediated by
> the object to be revealed, the most important factor is the development of a
> critical attitude in relation to the object and not a discourse by the educator
> about the object. And even when, in the midst of these relations, the educator
> and the learner come close to the object of their analysis and become curious
> about its meaning, they need the kind of solid information that is indispens-
> able to accurate analysis. To know is not to guess; information is useful only
> when a problem has been posed. Without this basic problem-statement, the
> furnishing of information is not a significant moment in the act of learn-
> ing and becomes simply the transfer of something from the educator to the
> learner. (p. 6)

It also surfaces when Freire provided guidance to the animators (adult
literacy workers) of the Culture Circles on how they should help community members to systematize their knowledge from their practice to develop
a critical understanding of their realities.

> As the teams are involved more and more deeply in a process of mutual learn-
> ing, they will discover that, on the one hand, they are the Subjects of that
> learning and, on the other hand, that the popular groups with whom they
> enter into dialogue are themselves the Subjects. Learning from and with these
> groups, the teams from the Center have a task from which they cannot escape

NEW DIRECTIONS FOR EVALUATION • DOI: 10.1002/ev

and for which they must be well prepared: that of helping, in the authentic sense of this word, the groups to analyze their praxis and to systematize their learning derived from this praxis. Thus they go beyond mere opinion about the facts to the critical comprehension of those same facts. (p. 44)

Freire's Pedagogical Principle 2: Consciousness Resides in Communities of People, Not Just Individuals

Throughout their work in Guinea-Bissau, members of the Idac team were extremely conscious about the need to involve the people in the communities in the design and implementation of any literacy effort. One basic strategy adopted in their work was to ensure the trained community animators would include community mobilization as an initial and essential part of their work with the local villagers. The mobilization, however, was not only to attract more people to participate in the cultural circles where the literacy efforts would take place; the villagers needed to become conscious about the importance of their educational processes and become co-owners or co-developers of such processes. The following is an example of those ideas provided by Freire in the context of explaining the successful work in Có village.

The Center's birth ... did not result only from the dream of the local animators team with the support from the Education Commissariat. In that team's dream there was the conviction that the Center could not just appear from nowhere as a gift given to the community. Therefore, the community should also assume the team's dream as something from their own ... This explains why the local animators did the initial political work involving the tabancas' committees. From the process of interpreting the project to make the Center a reality, the team would mobilize the people to actively participate in the first efforts to its creation. The joint work between the local people (who provided also their labor instruments) and the animators made it possible for the initial cleaning of the old army barrack and its surrounding fields."[1] (Freire, 1977)

Those ideas also surface when Freire explains how the literacy national program should be implemented in each community. He emphasizes it needed to be done through the establishment of a partnership with the local community political committees.

There is one point that it seems to me necessary to underline above all others. That is the "mass line" that characterizes the literacy work in the country. What is intended, fundamentally, is to see the literacy education of adults

---

[1] For some reason, this quoted paragraph presented in the original version of the book in Portuguese was not included in the English version of Freire's (1978) book *Pedagogy in Process: Letters to Guinea-Bissau*. Its translation has been provided by the authors from the original version of the book (Freire, 2001, pp. 49–51).

NEW DIRECTIONS FOR EVALUATION • DOI: 10.1002/ev

as a political act, coherent with the principles of PAIGC.[2] It is an act that informs the action of the government and is based on a real involvement of the people. Wherever programs of adult literacy are initiated, in accordance with the priorities established by the Party and the government, they are taken over, as far as possible, by the local population. In this way, an indispensable relation is established between the adult literacy programs and the political committees of the villages or city neighborhoods. Through these committees, the educators and local teachers, themselves activists, are put directly in touch with the people." (p. 50)

Freire's Pedagogical Principle 3: Critical Consciousness Pedagogy Must Be Interactive and Dialogical

Recognition and valuing of people's knowledge derived from their praxis was a basic principle Freire defended and practiced in any educational efforts he was involved with. He believed the act of knowing required from learners, complementary roles as creators, re-creators, and reinventors of the object of knowledge. They should be invited, triggered through their curiosity, to learn about existing knowledge while, at the same time, try to create new knowledge. If those two inseparable actions are disconnected, as he warned the Minister of Education team in Guinea-Bissau, it

> reduces the act of learning existing knowledge to mere bureaucratic transference. In such circumstances, the school, whatever its level, becomes a knowledge market; the professor, a sophisticated specialist who sells and distributes "packaged knowledge"; the learner, a client, who purchases and "consumes" this knowledge. (p. 6)

He also indicated that for them to promote a values-based education, there was a need for a complete detachment from the colonial system that saw the learners as passive receivers of standardized knowledge.

> An education that envisages making concrete such values as solidarity, social responsibility, creativity, discipline in the service of the common good, vigilance and a critical spirit—values by which PAIGC has been forged through the whole liberation process—would not be possible if, in that education, the learners continued to be what they were in the colonial educational system, mere recipients of packaged knowledge, transferred to them by their teachers. This latter process reduces them to mere "incidents" of the "educational" action of the educators." (p. 33)

---

[2] African Party for the Independence of Guinea and Cape Verde.

Freire's Pedagogical Principle 4: Integrate Reflection and Action

Members of the Idac team and of the Ministry of Education were able to put into practice Freire's idea of connecting theory and practice in any pedagogical, including literacy, efforts. Freire believed that Amilcar Cabral, the great leader and martyr of that country's war of independence, was an example of dialectically combining those concepts throughout his life.

> As with every person who truly lives out the coherence between political choice and actions, the word, for Cabral, was always a dialectical unity between action and reflection, practice and theory. He never allowed himself to be tempted on the one hand by empty words, nor on the other by activism. (p. 11)

The country's postindependence reality also required that Guinean students participate in the overall effort of national reconstruction. Therefore, school contents should be shaped based on current and concrete needs and not in aspects relevant only to the colonial power such as European geography. One of the programs they created as an attempt to address this issue was "Escola ao Campo" (the school to the country) that consisted of

> temporarily moving urban schools with their teachers and students to rural areas where, living in camps, they might learn with the peasants through participation in productive activities and also teach them some things, without in any way eliminating their regular school activities. (p. 14)

The project was expanded to gain national coverage in the following year (1976), contributing to the promotion of the integration between productive work and the normal school activities. Freire concludes that at some point "it becomes true that one no longer studies in order to work nor does one work in order to study; one studies in the process of working. There comes about, thus, a true unity between practice and theory" (p. 14). However, he stresses that this process does not eliminate analytic or critical thinking about practice, just the disconnection of those two essential concepts. Evaluation seminars upon the students' return from the countryside were held with the main objective of confirming, deepening or correcting the students' understanding of the themes and aspects discussed during the preparatory meetings prior to their departure (p. 15).

Freire's Pedagogical Principle 7: Critical Consciousness Pedagogy Is Co-Intentional Education Among Those Involved in Whatever Roles

Any pedagogical encounter not based on the idea of mutual learning, both for educators and educatees, was considered by Freire as oppressive practice, because it grows out of an ideology of domination. Therefore, from the beginning of their work in Guinea-Bissau, Idac members built their

NEW DIRECTIONS FOR EVALUATION • DOI: 10.1002/ev

relationship with the Ministry of Education as a partnership; they did not want to be the main subjects of the support they were asked to provide, nor did they wish to reduce the nationals as the mere objects of such support. They believed authentic support

> means that all who are involved help each other mutually, growing together in the common effort to understand the reality which they seek to transform. Only through such praxis—in which those who help and those who are being helped help each other simultaneously—can the act of helping become free from the distortion in which the helper dominates the helped. (p. 3)

Freire and his colleagues knew that they needed to be conscious that they were engaged in a dialectical relationship where they were learning from the Ministry's different teams' perspectives and, at the same time, being proactive in sharing with those partners their viewpoints and conclusions. Idac and the members of the Ministry teams should assume they were at the same time educators and educatees in their relationship.

> Naturally, while we were participants in the same process of decoding reality in dialogue with the national teams, we could not, on the one hand, be mere silent spectators nor, on the other, be the exclusive Subjects of the act of decoding … Actually, we found ourselves involved with the national teams in an act of knowing in which we, as much as they, had to assume the role of knowing Subjects … It would be through knowing and reknowing together that we would begin to learn and to teach together also. (p. 29)

Furthermore, they established strategies for collaborative analyses and syntheses about the reality concerned with the work they were doing. It was a continuous process of sharing Idac's perceptions and conclusions to be validated by the nationals, and then they had to go back to new analysis and synthesis.

> The recapitulation, which it was our task to initiate, meant that we must make clear the "reading" which we had made of national reality. Our "reading," in its turn, was put before the teams of the Commission on Education as a new challenge to which they must respond—either accepting it or rejecting it, totally or in part, improving it or deepening it. In the synthesis, we thus returned to the analysis, in order to reach a new synthesis. (p. 30)

In describing his perceptions about their visits to the project in Có Village, Freire indicated that the spirit of co-intentional education described above was clearly present within that project.

> In the dialectical unity between teaching and learning, the saying "Whoever knows, teaches the one who doesn't" takes on a revolutionary meaning. When

the one who knows understands first that the process by which he learned is social and, second, that in teaching something to another he is also learning something that he did not know already, then both are changed. This is the spirit one feels at Có. (p. 42)

Freire's Pedagogical Principle 8: Critical Consciousness Is Both Process and Outcome, Both Method and Result, and Both Analytical and Change-Oriented

Since the beginning of Idac's work in Guinea-Bissau, Freire and his colleagues had made it clear that the literacy campaign could not be an end in itself. It had to be done with high quality, but it should be directed toward the main challenge the country was facing at that time: reconstruct a nation from scratch. Therefore, the whole effort should be both focused on the quality of the campaign (process/method) and its ultimate contribution to that young nation (outcome/result).

> There would be no sense in transforming the emerging National Literacy Program for Adults into just one more campaign of the traditional type that we all know so well. Either through ingenuousness or artifice, all of these campaigns idealize literacy and give it a power that it does not, in itself, possess. The question facing the Guineans is not that of whether to do literacy education for its own sake or to do it as a means of transformation but, rather, how to put it at the service of national reconstruction. (pp. 21–22)

Freire's Pedagogical Principle 9: All Pedagogy Is Political

Upfront, Freire and his colleagues were well aware of the political role they were going to play in implementing the literacy program in Guinea-Bissau. They knew their work could not be just as of educational technicians. The job, as they saw it, required them to become believers and, even more, militants of the country's main cause of national rebuilding.

> We knew that we would be working not with cold objective intellectuals, nor with neutral specialists, but with militants engaged in a serious effort at reconstruction of their country... It is for this reason that only as militants could we become true collaborators, even in a very small way—never as neutral specialists or as members of a foreign technical assistance mission. (pp. 2–4)

In defining their roles, Freire generalizes that educators are at the same time "politicians" and "artists" as we could easily generalize also to the job of the evaluators. "The educator is a politician and an artist who must use the science of techniques but must never become a cold, neutral technician" (p. 21).

NEW DIRECTIONS FOR EVALUATION • DOI: 10.1002/ev

Freire's Pedagogical Principle 10: Critical Pedagogy Is Fundamentally Evaluative

Evaluative, critical thinking was embedded in all Freire's theories and methods. Collective and dialogical reflections about the job at hand, practice he called "permanent evaluation seminars," were the basic modus operandi for engaging key stakeholders of the literacy program in Guinea-Bissau. Evaluation seminars were held periodically by Idac as common practice to engage all the relevant stakeholders involved in the work in a dialogue to explore different views about what was working well, what could be improved and, most of all, the reasons why they were failing and find out what could be done to overcome the limitations.

> During a recent visit in September 1976 to the school at Có, we included trips to four small villages in the region. We were able to observe in the Culture Circles, held in the straw-roofed shelters, the extraordinary literacy work that was in progress there, growing out of the political-pedagogical presence of the school at Có. We also dedicated eight days of that trip to a seminar to evaluate all the work of the Commission. The evaluation, as mentioned earlier, does not consist of a process in which we take the Coordinating Commission and its work as the object of our analysis, discussing them with "professional airs." Rather, we and the Commission members together engage in dialogue about what is being done. We are active Subjects in the evaluation as we try to analyze together the cause of whatever failures there have been and to study alternative means of overcoming them. (p. 53)

The villagers were also engaged in processes of critical reflection about their achievements and challenges. He saw those encounters also as a key element to help the rural people start to think beyond their own villages and gain consciousness about their role in the reconstruction of their country.

> When people are able to see and analyze their own way of being in the world of their immediate daily life, including the life of their villages, and when they can perceive the rationale for the factors on which their daily life is based, they are enabled to go far beyond the narrow horizons of their own village and of the geographical area in which it is located, to gain a global perspective on reality. Political–pedagogical activity such as this—one that puts a dialectical theory of knowledge in practice—becomes, in itself, a fundamental dimension of the task of national reconstruction. (p. 45)

The Idac team also adopted strategies to reflect critically about the work conducted in the Culture Circles they had the opportunity of visiting. Seeing and listening, questioning and discussing were the basic tools they used to unveil whether the work of the local facilitators was really making a difference in empowering the people by helping them to develop critical consciousness through the literacy program.

> Obviously it was necessary that the five members of our team should be divided in order to visit at least some of the Culture Circles in action. At the stage at which we found ourselves—that of seeing and listening, asking and discussing, it was essential for us to observe how things were going in the Circles, among the participants and the literacy workers. We wanted to see both the creative aspects of their work and those instances where, on the contrary, they might be engaged merely in repetition and memorization. We were eager to know whether the learners had been able to appropriate for themselves their own "word," developing an ability to express themselves as conscious participants in a political act, or whether they were simply learning to read and write. (p. 19)

The Idac team also had internal seminars to evaluate their work. They had a sophisticated strategy for critically considering their perspectives in contrast with the perspectives from their national partners. Such a strategy would encompass decoding the given reality through their own lenses and/or trying to make this reflection by borrowing the analyses made by the nationals.

> In the first two phases, we looked on reality as a code that we were trying to decipher, sometimes with the national groups and sometimes among ourselves as a visiting team during our evaluation meetings while the work was in process. In this latter instance, we sometimes were engaged in a double task. Sometimes we took reality itself as the object of our analysis, attempting to "read it" critically. At other times, the object of our reflection was the process in which we had been engaged with the national teams when, with them, we had sought to analyze reality. In this way, we were analyzing the earlier analysis, trying to recapture critically the way in which we had perceived the same reality as the object of our curiosity. (p. 29)

Permanent evaluation seminars were proposed by the Idac team as the most important strategy for the local facilitators/animators to be more reflective about their work to identify what was not working and devise creative ways for improving their practice. Supervisors would also have a seat in those evaluation seminars to help foster and enrich discussions.

> The lack of such mistakes would really have surprised us, especially since the time given to training and theoretical formation of the workers had been so short. The ongoing process of the evaluation seminars would be a powerful force in overcoming these mistakes. Effective practices would be reinforced and errors eliminated. (p. 20)

NEW DIRECTIONS FOR EVALUATION • DOI: 10.1002/ev

Freire also defended the idea that people should exercise taking distance from their day-to-day operations as a way to make in-depth and more sound reflections to understand reality.

> It is on the basis of such a task that the Center is becoming a true university of the people. Both the teams and the groups take their own daily lives as the object of their reflection in a process of this nature. They are required to stand at a distance from the daily lives in which they are generally immersed and to which they often attribute an aura of permanence. Only at a distance can they get a perspective that permits them to emerge from that daily routine and begin their own independent development. The necessary precondition to taking a distance from "dailiness" is the analysis of past and present practice and the extension of this analysis into their possible future, remembering always that every practice is social in character. (pp. 44–45)

Potential Additional Freire's Pedagogical Principles Relevant to Evaluation Emerging from the Guinea-Bissau Experience

Our analyses of Freire and his colleagues' experience in Guinea-Bissau were based on the review of three written documents (Freire 1977, 1978; Idac, 1976) and on first-hand accounts from one of the members of the Idac team and co-author for this paper, Claudius Ceccon, who participated in the whole Guinea-Bissau experience with Freire. We have accessed references and information different than the ones Patton used to develop the list of his top 10 Freire's pedagogical principles with relevance to evaluation (see Chapter 3 of this volume). Therefore, it is not surprising that we have identified a couple of diverse, but complementary ideas that inspired us to discuss two possible additions to Patton's list.

Possible Freire's Pedagogical Principle 11: Experiences Are Not for Transplantation, They Are to Be Reinvented

Freire argued that there are no models that can be transplanted to other contexts without a critical assessment based on the specific characteristics of the specific context at hand.

> If there was anything that we discovered in Brazil that we were able to repeat exactly in Chile, it was not to separate the act of teaching from the act of learning. We also learned not to attempt to impose on the Chilean context what we had done in different circumstances in Brazil. Experiments cannot be transplanted; they must be reinvented. One of our most pressing concerns when we were preparing as a team for our first visit to Guinea-Bissau was to guard against the temptation to overestimate the significance of some aspect of an earlier experience, giving it universal validity. (pp. 4–5)

NEW DIRECTIONS FOR EVALUATION • DOI: 10.1002/ev

He went further by saying that this idea does not mean that one should not benefit from other experiences. Quite the reverse, past experiences should be seriously taken into consideration and serve as inspiration to reinvent what needs to be done in that new reality.

> On the contrary, what our past and present experiences teach us is that they cannot ever be simply transplanted. They can and must be explained, discussed and critically understood by those whose practice is in another context. In that new context they will be valid only to the degree that they are "reinvented." In this way, the experience which has happened in context A becomes valuable as an example for context B only if those working there re-create it, thus refusing the temptation to perform a mechanical and alienating transplant. Being completely closed to experiences realized in other contexts is just as wrong as being ingenuously open to them, leading to pure and simple importation. (p. 65)

The idea that, in order to be really relevant and helpful in a situation, an educator should not only bring preconceived models to make a direct transfer to any given context is completely applicable to evaluators and evaluations. Especially when we are dealing with complex programs (which most of them are!) an evaluator should be prepared to listen to each specific case and try to understand each unique reality—the context, the different players' interest and values, the politics around the program, etc. This is very much in line with Bob Stake's description of his well-known approach, responsive evaluation (Stake, 2004).

> Being responsive means orienting to the experience of personally being there, feeling the activity, the tension, knowing the people and their values. It relies heavily on personal interpretation. It gets acquainted with the concerns of stakeholders by giving extra attention to program action, to program uniqueness, and to the cultural plurality of the people. Its design usually develops slowly, with continuing adaptation of evaluation purpose and data gathering in pace with the evaluators becoming well acquainted with the program and its contexts. Some of this same experiential predisposition, determination to find "what's out there," can be built into any evaluation." (Stake, 2004, p. 86)

Developmental evaluation (DE; Patton, 2011) is another clear example that seems to have or could have been inspired by Freire's ideas of not trying to create and apply generalizable models to different realities. Patton's approach was developed for adaptive and emerging initiatives that are grounded in social change endeavors or other interventions functioning in uncertain, complex, and turbulent contexts. He indicates that the "[t]raditional evaluation approaches are not well suited for such turbulence... [they aim] to control and predict, to bring order to chaos" (p. 5). On the other hand, "[d]evelopment evaluation adapts to realities of complex nonlinear dynamics rather than trying to impose order and certainty on a disorderly and uncertain world" (p. 5).

Possible Freire's Pedagogical Principle 12: Root Any Pedagogical Effort in People's Real Interests and Needs, So Those Efforts Will Become More Effective

Freire believed that one of the most crucial aspects for a literacy effort to be successful was to connect the learning process to educatees' primary interests and needs. His adult literacy method was based in the establishment of generative words that learners were invited to break up to create new words through different combinations of syllables (Freire, 1970). For this process to be relevant to learners, the generative words as well as the new words created are supposed to be always directly related to a problem they are facing. This way, the learning process will have a meaning, be useful to people, and, therefore, have greater chances of success.

Throughout their work in Guinea-Bissau, Freire and his colleagues adopted strategies to ensure the literacy efforts being implemented in each village were grounded in the basic principles mentioned above. They engaged in several conversations with representatives from the ministries of education, agriculture, and health on how to connect the literacy program to other ongoing efforts involving production and health. This strategy would ensure exactly what Freire supported in his method: the literacy program will become more effective in helping learners conquer language by entering the scene as a systemic and relevant part of the main efforts for reconstructing the country (the problem at hand).

> Therefore, a major question confronting the Commission on Education, as the Commissioner so lucidly pointed out, is the inclusion of all of these concerns in adult-literacy projects. At the same time that students are learning reading and writing, they can, for example, consider their own practices with regard to the mosquito and the battle against malaria. Militant workers in production cooperatives, when they serve as literacy workers, can share their own experience regarding the advantages of mutual assistance in the accomplishment of work over individual efforts as the basis for establishing new cooperatives. In effective adult literacy education there is no place for exclusive categories of working and learning. The concerns of all of the different Commissions meet in the life of the people and can be incorporated into their process of learning and growing. (pp. 22–23)

This tentative pedagogical principle is closely aligned with some very important aspects of the evaluation discipline. Connecting the purposes of an evaluation with the real needs and priorities of key stakeholders or primary intended users of an evaluation is essential to ensure it will be relevant to the main issues of interest and, therefore, increase its use to inform deci-

NEW DIRECTIONS FOR EVALUATION • DOI: 10.1002/ev

sions and/or promote action (Bamberger, Rugh, & Mabry, 2012; Davidson, 2012; Patton, 1997). Furthermore, Scriven (2013) goes a bit further by indicating that the needs of the participants or users should be the primary source of values or of the criteria that will be used to determine merit and worth of a program or whatever else is being evaluated.

Closing Remarks

Even though frustrating at the end, given the political difficulties that impeded their efforts to continue, it is fair to say that Freire's experience in Guinea-Bissau was very rich and enlightening. It was a unique example of the application, adaptation, and reinvention of some of Freire's most noticeable aspects of his pedagogy. It corroborated most of the pedagogical principles with relevance to evaluation established by Patton (see Chapter 3 of this volume) and also illuminated a couple of new tentative complementary principles.

Freire teaches us through the Guinea-Bissau case that pedagogy is always in process. The act of teaching and learning is constantly being shaped by the political, economic, social, and cultural contexts and by who is playing the roles of educators and educatees. One aspect, however, that needs to be concomitantly present is that the pedagogical process needs to be always rooted in people's needs and primary interests, connected to a social change agenda.

Those ideas can and have been extrapolated to the evaluation arena by different and important authors, even if not explicitly sometimes. Evaluations are complex endeavors influenced deeply by the context as well as by the people involved. Models and approaches cannot really be transferred directly to other settings or even to the same setting in a different time, given changes in the context that always happen. Each evaluation process is unique and needs to be treated that way. Furthermore, to ensure quality, relevance and use, evaluations' purposes should be based on primary stakeholders' needs and priorities, which should also serve as a primary source of the values and criteria to be applied in the evaluation.

References

Bamberger, M., Rugh, J., & Mabry, L. (2012). *Realworld evaluation: Working under budget, time, data, and political constraints* (2nd ed.). Thousand Oaks, CA: Sage.

Brazil (1964). *Institui o Programa Nacional de Alfabetização do Ministério da Educação e Cultura e dá outras providências*. Decreto No. 53.465, de 21 de Janeiro de 1964. Diário Oficial da União—Seção 1—22/1/1964, Página 629 (Publicação Original).

Davidson, E. J. (2012). *Actionable evaluation basics: Getting succinct answers to the most important questions* [Kindle iPad version] (2nd version; revised September 25, 2012). Retrieved from http://www.amazon.com.br.

Fetterman, D. M. (2001). *Foundations of empowerment evaluation*. Thousand Oaks, CA: Sage.

Freire Institute. (n.d.). *Concepts used by Paulo Freire*. Burnley, United Kingdom: Frere Institute. Retrieved from http://www.freire.org/component/easytagcloud/118-module/conscientization/
Freire, P. (1970). *Pedagogy of the oppressed*. New York, NY: Herder & Herder.
Freire, P. (1977). *Cartas à Guiné-Bissau: Registros de uma experiência em progresso* (4a ed.). Rio de Janeiro, Brazil: Paz e Terra.
Freire, P. (1978). *Pedagogy in process: The letters to Guinea Bissau*. New York, NY: The Seabury Press.
House, E. R., & Howe, K. R. (1999). *Values in evaluation and social research*. Thousand Oaks, CA: Sage.
Idac (Institute for Cultural Action). (1976). *Guinea-Bissau: Reinventing education*. Document Idac Series 11/12. Geneva, Switzerland: Institute for Cultural Action.
Patton, M. Q. (1997). *Utilization-focused evaluation: The new century text* (3rd ed.). Thousand Oaks, CA: Sage.
Patton, M. Q. (2011). *Developmental evaluation: Applying complexity concepts to enhance innovation and use*. New York, NY: The Gilford Press.
Pelandré, N. L. (2002). *Ensinar e aprender com Paulo Freire: 40 horas, 40 anos depois*. São Paulo, Brazil: Cotez.
Scriven, M. (1994). *Evaluation thesaurus* (4th ed.). Newbury Park, CA: Sage.
Scriven, M. (2013). *Key evaluation checklist (KEC)*. Retrieved from http://www.michaelscriven.info/images/KEC_3.22.2013.pdf
Stake, R. E. (2004). *Standards-based and responsive evaluation*. Thousand Oaks, CA: Sage.

THOMAZ CHIANCA *is an international evaluation consultant with 20 years of experience in Brazil and in 24 other countries. He runs his own successful evaluation coaching, training, and consulting practice, COMEA Relevant Evaluations. He is a dental surgeon at the Federal University of Rio de Janeiro, where he teaches research methods to graduate students and supports research and extension projects. He has a Ph.D. in interdisciplinary evaluation from Western Michigan University (USA) and is a founding member of the Brazilian Monitoring and Evaluation Association and a member of the Fast Forward Fund (3F) managing board.*

CLAUDIUS CECCON *is the Executive Director of the Center for the Creation of People's Image, a nongovernmental organization based in Rio de Janeiro that produces educational audio-visual and printed toolkits, conceives public interest campaigns, and organizes training courses and seminars for educators and social actors, empowering and qualifying their action as citizens in bringing about necessary changes to improve democracy in our society. He is also well known as a political cartoonist and illustrator. Claudius and Paulo Freire were political allies and were exiled from Brazil at the same time of the work described in this chapter.*

NEW DIRECTIONS FOR EVALUATION • DOI: 10.1002/ev

Guimarães, V. (2017). Transformative pedagogical evaluation: Freirean principles practiced in Brazilian public schools. In M. Q. Patton (Ed.), *Pedagogy of Evaluation. New Directions for Evaluation, 155*, 99–110.

5

Transformative Pedagogical Evaluation: Freirean Principles Practiced in Brazilian Public Schools

Vilma Guimarães

Abstract

In Brazil, the evaluation that is currently practiced in schools has been promoting the failure of the poorest, who eventually interrupt their studies, convinced of their incompetence. This article shows that, in contrast, hundreds of schools across the country adopt a cooperative dialogical pedagogy of evaluation. As part of an approach based on Freirean principles, the Telessala Methodology teaches students who are discriminated against by the traditional school, that they are smart and creative, with power to change their lives and the world. This chapter describes the Telessala Methodology and how it manifests the principles of Freirean pedagogy with implications for evaluation. © 2017 Wiley Periodicals, Inc., and the American Evaluation Association.

Personal Context

Allow me to start with a personal note, to justify the focus of my reflections in this chapter: the contrast between the colonizing pedagogy of evaluation embedded in the evaluation culture that still prevails in most educational institutions and the liberating possibilities of Freirean pedagogy, making evident that educational innovations such as

NEW DIRECTIONS FOR EVALUATION, no. 155, Fall 2017 © 2017 Wiley Periodicals, Inc., and the American Evaluation Association. Published online in Wiley Online Library (wileyonlinelibrary.com) • DOI: 10.1002/ev.20258

the *Telessala Methodology*[1] can promote a transformative evaluation that affirms the citizen's humanity and so contributes to build social equity and justice.

I am what Schon calls a "reflective practitioner," an educator who follows the motto of the great Galileo Galilei: *"thinking and acting, on the action again to think, and so to walk."* Still a teenager, I experienced the same political–cultural atmosphere in which the adult Paulo Freire lived. I was aware of his ideas and of the Culture Circles[2] he was organizing, and decided to act accordingly. Since 1970, while working as a principal in Pernambuco State's public schools, I've challenged, in practice, the dominant education and evaluation models, presenting alternatives. Two decades later, as Roberto Marinho's Foundation[3] Education Manager, I've participated in the creation and implementation of the Telessala Methodology, a vast collective enterprise that on several occasions had the personal participation of Paulo Freire, and, after his death in 1997, the involvement of the Institute that bears his name (see Chapter 1 in this volume).

I want to discuss here this methodology, adopted in most Brazilian states in 1995 as public educational policy. It has been successfully used in public schools and other institutions, such as hospitals, prisons, and companies, making of education "an act of love, and therefore of courage, which does not fear the debate, the reality analysis, the creative discussion"(Freire, 1969, p. 95). In the pages that follow I'll try to answer the question that opens this *New Directions* volume: *"What is your pedagogy of evaluation?"* In so doing I'll share a story that only a few know: how the meeting of individuals and institutions committed to social change has, little by little, shaped an approach that develops critical evaluative thinking and expresses, in its components, the Freirean principles relevant to a transformative pedagogy of evaluation, conceptualized and discussed by Patton in Chapter 3 of this volume.

---

[1] The Telessala Methodology was systematized in the book *Include to transform: Telessala methodology in five movements* (Guimarães, 2013). The name *Telessala*, formed by the conjunction of "Tele" (television) and "sala" (room), the physical space, is justified because the approach has become popularly known for promoting the use of TV and computers in the classrooms, at a time when the presence of ICT in educational systems was scarce.
[2] Culture Circles were meetings generally conducted with the participants arranged in circle, in which Paulo Freire and his team held dialogues with peasants, using images as triggers of a reflection about their reality.
[3] The Roberto Marinho Foundation was established in 1977 by the journalist Roberto Marinho, founder of the organizations that today form the *Globo Group*, moved by his commitment to social responsibility. Roberto Marinho's belief that communication can be an instrument of social change was sustained by his heirs, who are now the Foundation's maintainers. This institution creates, develops, and implements, in all Brazil, projects in education, historical heritage, and culture.

A Look at Educational Evaluation That Excludes and Its Alternative

In many countries of the so-called "Global South," for too much time, educational evaluation remained tied to a colonizing education model centered on the transmission of information disconnected from practice, serving the maintenance of an oppressive status quo. It manifests the "banking" concept of education, defined and criticized by Freire in his *Pedagogy of the Oppressed*. Colonizing education is characterized by disregarding the knowledge that is specific to every nation and community. It attempts to standardize the rich cultural diversity of the planet and of each region within the different countries. Centered on school education, its purpose is not to enable the creation of new knowledge, but to stimulate the repetition of knowledge produced in other contexts and so to perpetuate dependency and submission. Brazilian educational culture is still impregnated with this colonizing paradigm.[4]

Consistent with the principles of a colonizing education, traditional evaluation establishes top-down abstract patterns to which all must adjust. It abhors differences and considers the students' mistakes as deviations from the norm, which should be corrected and punished. The educational system, like the penal system, nurtures the belief that punishment has a positive educational effect and contributes to the individual's "recovery," persuading him or her not to repeat the mistake. In schools, the punishment is given through low grades that lead to retention. The word "retention" in Portuguese is "reprovação", meaning "disapproval," and its etymology refers to "ordeal" (*provação*) and "trial" (*prova*). Our experience shows, however, that punishment does not educate anybody. What generates personal change is a wholesome humanizing educational process.

Almost all children and young people who fail at Brazilian schools tend to decline in performance after each year of retention. Their self-confidence and self-esteem are hindered. They are mostly black, Indians, or blue collar workers, and, as a rule, belong to the poorest families. Feeling rejected by school, they drop out, without completing the basic education to which they are entitled.[5]

---

[4] On the concept of colonizing education, see *Schooling the world* (https://www.youtube.com/watch?v=6t_HN95-Urs) and *Forbidden education* (https://www.youtube.com/watch?v=-t60Gc00Bt8#t=2400). The difficulty of Brazilian education in breaking its ties with the colonizing paradigm has historical roots. After all, until 1822 the country was a vassal of Portugal. In 1888, when slavery finally was abolished, only about 10% had rights as citizens. In 1889 Brazil became a Republic and stopped being ruled by an emperor with blood ties to the Portuguese royal family.

[5] Research in Brazil, like that conducted by the Carlos Chagas Foundation–Sao Paulo, confirms the relationship between retention, school drop-out, and the hindering of the new generation's future. Students who are retained are much more likely to quit school. See also *Alternatives to grade retention*—Shane Jimerson,

The Essence of a Transformative Evaluation

In his recollections of his time (1930s) as a student in the "public school meant for few," Paulo Freire tells about a teacher who did not use evaluation to humiliate and tame the children, but to validate their competence and encourage them to continue learning. Paulo, then a shy boy, "feeling ugly and less capable than the others," coyly submitted an essay to the master. After reading the text, the teacher stood by the side of the future author of *Pedagogy of the Oppressed* and communicated with his body language that the boy had produced something of value and had a great potential (Freire, 2008, p. 43).

The attitude of that teacher points to the essence of a transformative evaluation—it is made with the learners, in their benefit, never against them. It contributes to empower them, to increase their ability to act. The insecure teenager grew up to create the revolutionary method that, in the early 1960s, would alphabetize, in 40 hours, 300 peasants in the city of Angicos, Rio Grande do Norte, who were invited to "read first the world, then the word," a feat that would lead him to prison and exile in 1964.

Inspired by Freire

During the years Freire was forced to live abroad (authoritarian regimes fear those who teach to think), I and other young people were reading on the sly his books *Education as the Practice of Freedom* (Freire, 1968) and *Pedagogy of the Oppressed* (Freire, 1974). By then, it was very clear to me and many of my colleagues that the Freirean approach was not just a method of adult literacy: it was also a new theory of education, that put in check oppressive traditional schooling. Although in 1970 the school was regarded as an institution representing the capitalist state, where popular education could not flourish, I have always believed in the contradictions that make it possible to introduce and develop, in public schools, practices that are at the service of the majority of the population they serve.

Therefore, as a principal of public schools located in poor communities near Recife, Brazil,[6] my team and I started putting into practice Freire's teachings about the insolvable association between education, communication, and culture; about dialogue as the foundation of educative interactions; and about the importance of raising awareness on the fact that we are not just products but also producers of culture. In spite of the dictatorial government we were living under, popular democratic educational processes were implemented in these schools.

Sarah Platcher, Mary-Ella Kerr; Counseling, 2005, p. 11 (http://www.nasponline.org/resources/principals/Retention%20WEB.pdf).
[6] School Frei Caneca, in the municipality of Camaragibe and Polyvalent School Composer Antonio Maria, in Olinda.

It was then that we realized that the traditional evaluation tools were insufficient to grasp how students were building knowledge, new attitudes and behaviors, and increased power to act. We thought about the essence of the evaluation in Freire's Culture Circles, the peasants' self-evaluation, and in a collective that included the Circle's coordinators, and discovered what they had learnt. Then, we intuitively came to the conclusion that, to be consistent with a Freirean approach, evaluation should be based on dialogue.

In this way, we've created new ways to evaluate, which went beyond the written or oral tests. The students presented to parents and the community what they had learned, using different languages, such as art, dance, and drama, and received feedback. Class councils were organized, with the participation of parents and with students' representation, to discuss the results achieved. Children and young people were perceived in a holistic way, considering that the human being's cognitive, emotional, and spiritual dimensions are inseparable. So, we went way beyond assigning numeric values from 0 to 10 marking student progress. The heart of the matter was to help the students to realize how much they had already walked toward their goals and give them confidence to move on.

New Opportunity

In 1979, thanks to the government's democratic revitalization that ensured amnesty to the regime's political prisoners, Paulo Freire was allowed to return to Brazil, and our paths would cross again. But before reporting this reunion, connected to the history of the Telessala Methodology, I want to note here that Paulo Freire was a pioneer in the fight to neutralize, in public education systems, the evaluation that teaches the poorest that they are responsible for their own misery because they are "unable to learn."

The experience of Paulo Freire in São Paulo city Education Department (1989–1991)[7] has shown that it is possible to carry out, under the aegis of the state, a popular education characterized by an emancipatory policy, guided by the principles of dialogue, citizen's participation and democratic management (see Gadotti, Chapter 1 of this volume). In this context, educators were invited to rethink their conceptions of evaluation and make it an intrinsic part of the learning process, not only of the students, but of themselves and other educational leaders.

As a strategy to limit the damage caused by the selective and exclusionary character of evaluation, the elementary school system abandoned grade levels replaced by continuous progression learning cycles, in the course of which the student could not be retained (Saul, 2009). By the end of the

---

[7] Although Freire decided to leave the City Department of Education in 1991, the Freirean Project lasted until 1993 in São Paulo municipality, with his friends Mario Sergio Cortella and Moacir Gadotti as, respectively, Secretary and Chief of Staff.

1990s, inspired by what Paulo Freire had done in the capital, São Paulo State public elementary schools, then with eight grades, began to be organized in in two cycles of continuous progression and learning (Cycle 1, first to fourth grades; and Cycle 2, fifth to eighth grades). Children, although continuously evaluated, could not be retained for "bad performance." In 1998, the São Paulo State Board of Education adopted the system of cycles for all São Paulo State elementary schools, both public and private.

Paulo Freire and the Telessala Methodology

Collective work, an assumption of education as social practice, is a central principle in Freire's work (see Chapter 1 of this volume). And so was the building of the Telessala Methodology. It was born of a collective, organic, evolutionary process, which developed over time, even before we were aware of it. Its pre-history began when Silke Weber, who had collaborated with educator Paulo Freire in the Culture Circles, was named Minister of Education of Pernambuco State (1987–1990). Paulo Freire became a consultant of the Department of Adult and Youth's Education in that Secretariat at the same time I took over the direction of its Department of Educational Technology. There, with a committed team of professionals, we explored the educational potential of television and videos. Initially, we used them as a technology for face-to-face and distance training of educators in Pernambuco. Based on Freirean principles, we gradually developed a strategy of *image's reading* that we began to apply when using the *Telecurso*,[8] which was, at that time, a set of video programs and textbooks for at-distance education, created by the Roberto Marinho Foundation. We also used other educational television programs to strengthen the pedagogical practice of public school educators "from the outback to the pier."[9] In addition, the Telecurso was used to enable young people and adults who could not afford to finish basic education on schedule because of the aforementioned characteristics of traditional schooling and evaluation, to complete with quality their studies at primary and secondary levels.

The stage for my reunion with Paulo Freire was set; he went on to advise the Department of Educational Technology, lending his image and speech to educational programs that we produced.

The partnership between the Department of Educational Technology and Roberto Marinho Foundation eventually resulted in an invitation for me to assume that entity's Education Management Office. In 1992, in that

---

[8] The Telecurso, officially acknowledged by the Brazilian Ministry of Education—MEC, is the largest and most significant achievement of Fundação Roberto Marinho in the area of education. By 2015, seven million students had completed its program, which is adopted in most Brazilian states.

[9] This expression, used extensively in Pernambuco, a coastal state, means an action that covers the entire region, from the outback (*sertã*) to the litoral (the *cais*, or pier).

NEW DIRECTIONS FOR EVALUATION • DOI: 10.1002/ev

new position, I built the team, through my educational career contacts in the public school system of Pernambuco, of professionals united around the approach articulated in Freire's books *Education as Practice of Freedom* (1968) and *Pedagogy of the Oppressed* (1974).

I was already working at the Roberto Marinho Foundation, and I accompanied Paulo Freire in his emotional return to Angicos, in Rio Grande do Norte State. He brought with him a group of old and new collaborators. Thirty years had gone by since the innovative Freirean experience of adult literacy had been interrupted in 1964. Paulo's moving reunion with old women and men who had participated in the Culture Circles as learners and coordinators was registered and resulted in four television programs for the *Globo Science* series.

The presence of a group inspired by progressive ideas in the Roberto Marinho Foundation's Education Management Office made possible a larger role for its educational materials. In 1995, a new version of Telecurso's videos and books was launched with a more comprehensive content, aiming at those willing either to complete elementary school or high school, or receive vocational training. Also, a framework was created to implement educational projects using the Telecurso materials.

Between 1996 and 1997, Paulo accepted Roberto Marinho Foundation's invitation to create a new Telecurso series that would be called *Weaving the Knowledge*, aimed at young people and adults who, although not illiterate, needed to attend the initial classes of elementary school. Having cordinated and followed up the design and production of the Telecurso's new edition, my team and I succeeded in systematizing its use in classrooms by interested educators: the Telessala Methodology. This methodology uses the Freirean principle that *"critical consciousness is interactive and dialogic"* (Chapter 3 of this volume) to build cooperative learning communities, where the educational technology, represented by Telecurso's videos and books, is used in the context of a problematizing approach.

With its pedagogical proposal focused on the world of work, on the development of skills and on Citizenship Education, the Telessala Methodology implementation has proven to diminish school dropouts, to eliminate grade retention, and to increase teacher and student performance, because the learning of the first reflects and influences the learning of the second. Moreover, the Telessala Methodology promotes critical thinking, leading to projects of change toward more fair and sustainable realities, thus allowing that Freirean principle to be put into practice in public education systems from North to South of Brazil.

The book *Include to Transform: Telessala Methodology in Five Movements* presents the theoretical foundation of the approach, including the concept of Cultural Hegemony from Gramsci, Edgar Morin's Complex Thought, Moacir Gadotti's Pedagogy of the Earth, and highlights Paulo Freire's conceptions of education and culture as an articulating axis (Guimarães, 2013, pp. 86–115). The same book identifies the components of the methodology, which are interrelated in order to produce learning and systemic change (pp. 5–6). I'll highlight some of what was produced: curricular organization, production and use of materials, organization of situational learning, training of educators, and evaluation. In the remainder of this chapter, I will give examples of their connection to Freirean principles identified by Patton in Chapter 3 of this volume. Each individual component of the methodology can express all the principles, given the articulation and interdependence of both Freirean principles and the methodological components addressed. However, for reasons of space, in most cases I will confine myself to illuminating each principle.

Telessala Methodology and the Freirean Principles as Pedagogy of Evaluation

Principle 1. "Use Evaluative Thinking to Open Up, Develop, and Nurture Critical Consciousness" (Patton, Chapter 3, this volume)

Evaluative thinking examines the assumptions of the information received, considers its contradictions and inconsistencies, articulates values, and deals with complexity. This nurtures critical conscience, which allows people to make sense of reality itself, to better act on it. The curriculum of both Telecurso and Telessala Methodology is aligned with this principle and stimulates evaluative thinking because it deals with knowledge in an interdisciplinary contextualized perspective. "The main themes of each module of the pedagogical work are interconnected to form individuals who think, who know themselves, know their circumstances and are able to intervene on them; who discover and live their condition of citizens" (Guimarães, 2013, p. 118). Such themes are introduced by questions, to be answered by the students through the lens/perspectives of each discipline: Who am I? (Module 1); Where am I? (Module 2); Where I am going? (Module 3); and What is my mission in the world? (Module 4).

Principle 2. "Consciousness Resides in Communities of People, Not Just in Individuals"

"Nobody educates nobody, nobody educates himself or herself. People educate each other in community, with the world as a mediator," says the Pedagogy of the Oppressed (Freire, 2015, p. 95). By educating each other, they develop critical awareness and become more and more human. In the Telessala Methodology, the production and use of educational materials respect this principle. The format of the videos (telelessons) and accompanying publications leads to overcoming isolation by inviting the group of students to perform a collective reading of reality. Each 15-minute telelesson represents a codification of the students' reality, similar to that in 1993 by Brennand, at the request of Freire. This artist from Pernambuco produced posters where basic concepts related to the life experiences of the peasants who participated in the Culture Circles were visually encoded. These images were the element that triggered the analysis and problematization of reality by the group (the *decoding*, facilitated by a popular educator). In the Telessala Methodology, the video encodes, in the *scene–text*,[10] challenging situations, the goal of which is to stimulate curiosity and provoke reflection. When decoded collectively by the group, it enables the students, for example, to become conscious of their values and beliefs, often biased, or of the political and social forces that are behind unfair situations considered "natural."

To assist students in realizing they are producers and products of the culture of their region and can integrate it in the educational projects they develop, *Copybooks of Culture* are published, to "expose the art, customs, beliefs and the people of the States in which the Telessala Methodology is experienced" (Guimarães, 2013, p. 132).

Principles 3, 5, and 6. "Critical Conscience Is Interactive and Dialogic"; "Value the Objective and the Subjective"; "Integrate Thought and Emotion"

In order to develop critical thinking and to be able to deconstruct stereotypical and biased views of reality that perpetuate oppression, it is necessary to overcome the banking education model and understand that learning can happen only through dialogue between people who are different. Dialogue creates intersubjectivity, which surpasses the dichotomy between objectivity and subjectivity, between thought and emotion, generating knowledge and affection—and both are the result of human interactions. Freirean principles 3, 5, and 6 can be recognized in the *organization of learning* of the Telessala Methodology. The teacher, acting as pedagogical mediator, uses technology and a variety of educational materials, with the aim of promoting dialogue between all members of the group and to make learning more affective, effective, and intense. Daily routine includes the organization of the group into teams, social integration activities, questioning/problematization, reading images, teamwork, learning socialization, and learning evaluation.

One of the more fruitful procedures to develop the socio-emotional and intellectual skills of the group is to split it into teams so that each team is responsible for an aspect of the pedagogical work. These teams change periodically, so everyone has the opportunity to experience each one of the aspects. The Socialization team organizes activities that promote integration, solidarity, sharing, and affectivity, seeking to strengthen ties. The Integration team promotes social and artistic activities to increase trust in the group, a fundamental ingredient to foster dialogue. The Coordination team

---

[10] Scene–text (*Cenatexto*, in Portuguese) is the story/narrative through which the topic to be discussed by the group in a given class is problematized.

assists in the planning and organization of classes, so materials and time can be well used. The Synthesis team has the task of systematizing and presenting the most important points of the learning built during the day, and there is also the Assessment team. It is responsible for promoting, at the end of the activities, a moment of collective reflection, focusing on the theme that was developed, the material used, the dynamics, the role of the teacher mediator, and the involvement of the students.

In the Telessala Methodology, the place of affection (emotion) is as important as the place of Science: The warm social atmosphere favors the construction of scientific knowledge because this warmth supports recognition and appreciation of differences, and respect for the beliefs and values of others, facilitating the exchange of knowledge, essential to the development of new concepts (Guimarães, 2013, p. 139).

Principle 4. "Integrating Reflection and Action"

Patton points out that for Freire, reflection is directed to action and action is the content of reflection (Chapter 3 of this volume). In educational settings, the student must be constantly invited to reflect on the activities performed, whether at school or outside it. Teacher training in the Telessala Methodology is guided by this principle. The professional development process provides that the teacher develops the same skills that students need to develop and become reflective practitioners. In weekly or biweekly meetings they evaluate their practice and plan their lessons. They reflect on the results achieved. While revisiting their practice in a collective, systematic way, they can identify the learning needs of the students and of themselves (Guimarães, 2013, p. 141). In this way, professionals who are responsible for the Telessala Methodology Teachers Training component, such as Madalena Freire (an educator, Freire's daughter), have been producing theoretical texts that invite the teacher to become "a thinking educator, a researcher of his or her teaching, capable of the disciplined exercise of reflection on practice and theory, combined with observation, evaluation, and planning practices" (Guimarães, 2013, p. 139).

Principle 10. "Critical Pedagogy Is Fundamentally and Continuously Evaluative"

In a problematizing education, learners "develop their power of grasping and understanding the world, which appears in their relationships with it, no longer as a static reality, but as a reality in transformation, in process" (Freire, 2015, p. 100). In other words, they develop critical consciousness through a continued reflection about what they think, feel, and do, which is nothing more than to compare theory and practice, to discuss and question judging criteria, and evaluate. The evaluation that is practiced in Telessala Methodology expresses a critical pedagogy, because it teaches thinking: to think as a group, in a participatory, dialogic way.

Evaluation within Telessala Methodology is horizontal, participatory, dialogic, transparent, and continuous, an invitation to all those involved in the educational process to develop self-knowledge and take responsibility for promoting their own learning. It is an essential part of their reflection on the practice, indispensable to foster learning and change. It is a continuous formative process that makes it possible to diagnose situations, illuminating the road already traveled, and empowering everyone involved in the direction of more transformative actions. Thus it leads to strengthening citizenship and democracy. It is, in short, to "think the practice as the best way to improve practice. Thinking about the practice in which theory is embedded. The evaluation of the practice as a way of promoting theoretical formation" (Freire, 2001b, p. 11).

The Telessala Methodology evaluation respects the right to learn. So the teachers learn to evaluate the students in all their potential, using their sensitivity and ability to capture evidence of advancement and signs of concern. In addition, teachers learn to self-evaluate as educators, to evaluate the school and the larger educational context, which are inseparable from the social and economic dimensions of educational life. The students, in turn, also learn to self-evaluate and evaluate others, giving and receiving feedback. They discover the importance of evaluating context as part of making decisions about their own lives. Advances and difficulties, as well as value judgments about their personal growth and the group's growth, are recorded in a portfolio (known as *Memorial* in Portuguese). With regard to developing evaluative competencies and skills, the students' participation in the Evaluation team enables the development of essential skills for those who want to change reality: observation, self-criticism, and comparison between the planned and the accomplished as a basis for decision making.

Conclusion: A Pedagogy of Evaluation for Social Justice

The pedagogy of evaluation of the Telessala Methodology is inspired by Freirean principles that seek to establish a world without oppressors and oppressed. It targets the poor and marginalized to enhance their power to transform their lives and the world.

Between 1995 and 2015, Telessala Methodology and Freire's pedagogy of the evaluation enabled 7 million young people and adults (who otherwise would still be believing that they were inferior to others and unable to learn) to complete an emancipatory, empowering basic education. With the Telessala Methodology, those who are confined in prisons and hospitals, or reside in areas difficult to access in the countryside, on Indian reservations, or lands of former slaves (*quilombos*), do not run the risk of being excluded from the right to education or being prevented from completing their studies.

Brazilian public schools that apply the Telessala Methodology are invited to produce concrete examples of learning through dialogue.

Educators in these schools understand that *another evaluation is possible*: ethical, democratic, and participatory, where decisions about what will be evaluated and how it will be evaluated are taken in a collective way. Evaluation is continuous, occurring throughout the learning process, enabling those involved to act and reflect on the action taken, celebrate the positive results, and consider the mistakes as opportunities for learning and growth.

"Principles are hypotheses, not truths. They may or may not work. They may or may not be followed. They may or may not lead to desired outcomes. Whether they work, whether they are followed, and whether they yield desired outcomes are subject to evaluation" (Chapter 3 of this volume). External evaluations of Telecurso and the Telessala Methodology carried out in educational systems by states and municipalities, like those in Pernambuco, Acre, and Rio de Janeiro, for example, are demonstrating that, *Yes*, Freirean principles work. The data collected and interpreted indicate the power of the Telessala Methodology virtually to eliminate dropouts and enable students to progress appropriate to their ages. Thus, Telecurso and Telessala Methodology perform their mission to include in order to transform, toward the fair and sustainable country that we envision.

References

Freire, P. (1968). *Education as the practice of freedom.* New York: Rowland & Littlefield.
Freire, P. (1974). *Pedagogy of the oppressed.* New York: Bloomsbury.
Freire, P. (1969). *Pedagogia como prática da liberdade.* Rio de Janeiro, Brazil: Civilização Brasileira.
Freire, P. (2001a). *Pedagogia da autonomia.* São Paulo, Brazil: Paz e Terra.
Freire, P. (2001b). *Política e educação: Ensaios* (Coleção Questões de Nossa Época, Vol. 23). São Paulo, Brazil: Cortez.
Freire, P. (2015). *Pedagogia do oprimido.* São Paulo, Brazil: Paz e Terra.
Guimarães, V. (org. Incluir para Transformar). (2013). *Metodologia Telessala em cinco movimentos.* Rio de Janeiro, Brazil: Fundação Roberto Marinho.
Saul, A. M. (2009). O legado de Paulo Freire para as políticas de currículo e para a formação de educadores no Brasil. *Revue. Brasil Est Pedagogia.*, Brasília, *90*(224), 223–244.

VILMA GUIMARÃES *is General Manager of Education and Implementation of the Roberto Marinho Foundation, Rio de Janeiro, Brazil. She is responsible for the pedagogical conception of technological innovations and the implementation of the Foundation's educational projects. She was a teacher, pedagogical coordinator, and school director in the Department of Educational Technology of the State Secretariat of Education of Pernambuco.*

NEW DIRECTIONS FOR EVALUATION • DOI: 10.1002/ev

Fetterman, D. (2017). Transformative empowerment evaluation and Freirean pedagogy: Alignment with an emancipatory tradition. In M. Q. Patton (Ed.), *Pedagogy of Evaluation*. *New Directions for Evaluation, 155*, 111–126.

6

Transformative Empowerment Evaluation and Freirean Pedagogy: Alignment With an Emancipatory Tradition

David Fetterman

Abstract

Empowerment evaluation and Freirean pedagogy share a common emancipatory tradition. These approaches help people learn to confront the status quo, by questioning assumptions and prescribed roles, unpacking myths, rejecting dehumanization, and no longer blindly accepting the "truth" about how things are or can be. They help people think critically about the world around them. © 2017 Wiley Periodicals, Inc., and the American Evaluation Association.

E mpowerment evaluation and Freirean pedagogy are both forms of transformative education. They create environments conducive to people empowering themselves. They rely on cycles of reflection and action to contribute to transformation. They both attack the "culture of silence" (acquiescence to a pervasive system of beliefs that undermine and devalue entire groups of people). Empowerment evaluation and Freirean pedagogy share a common belief that:

> Every person, however … submerged in the "culture of silence," can look critically at his or her world through a process of dialogue with others, and can gradually come to perceive his personal and social reality, think about it, and take action in regard to it. (Shaull, 1974, p. 13)

This stands in juxtaposition to educational approaches that are designed to reproduce the status quo. As Shaull (1974) explains:

> There is no such thing as a neutral educational process. Education either functions as an instrument which is used to facilitate integration of the younger generation into the logic of the present system and bring about conformity or it becomes the practice of freedom, the means by which men and women deal critically and creatively with reality and discover how to participate in the transformation of their world. (p. 15)

Empowerment evaluation and Freirean pedagogy are both dedicated to the concepts of community and collaboration, as well as self-determination, social justice, and sustainability. Empowerment evaluation and Freirean pedagogy are aligned in principle and practice. I was influenced by Freirean pedagogy before developing empowerment evaluation, while breathing life into the approach, and continue to be influenced by his work into the present.

The Niche of Empowerment Evaluation

Empowerment evaluation is a stakeholder-involvement approach to evaluation. It differs from other similar stakeholder-involvement approaches in the following manner: collaborative evaluators are in charge of the evaluation; participatory evaluators jointly share control of the evaluation; and empowerment evaluators view program staff members, program participants, and community members as in control of the evaluation (Fetterman, Rodriguez-Campos, Wandersman, & Goldfarb O'Sullivan, 2014).

Empowerment evaluation is the use of evaluation concepts, techniques, and findings to foster improvement and self-determination (Fetterman, 1994). It is an approach that "aims to increase the likelihood that programs will achieve results by increasing the capacity of program stakeholders to plan, implement, and evaluate their own programs" (Wandersman et al., 2005, p. 28). It is mainstreamed as part of the planning and management of the program/organization. In essence, empowerment evaluation is a tool to help people produce desired outcomes and reach their goals.

Two Streams

Empowerment evaluation in practice is typically applied along two streams. The first is practical and the second transformative. Practical empowerment evaluation is similar to formative evaluation. It is designed to enhance program performance and productivity. It is still controlled by program staff, participants, and community members. However, the focus is on practical problem solving, as well as programmatic improvements and outcomes.

NEW DIRECTIONS FOR EVALUATION • DOI: 10.1002/ev

Transformative empowerment evaluation (Fetterman, 2015) highlights the psychological, social, and political power of liberation. People learn how to take greater control of their own lives and the resources around them. The focus in transformative empowerment evaluation is on liberation from predetermined, conventional roles and organizational structures or "ways of doing things." In addition, empowerment is a more explicit and apparent goal. Freirean pedagogy is most closely aligned with transformative empowerment evaluation in that it is committed to helping people confront the culture of silence about the status quo, raise consciousness about their role in the world (as compared with "false consciousness"[1]), and improve the human condition.

Theories

Reviewing the theories guiding empowerment evaluation practice will also help illuminate the integral relationship between Freirean pedagogy and empowerment evaluation: empowerment theory, self-determination theory, evaluation capacity building, process use, and theories of use and action.

Empowerment Theory

This theory is about gaining control, obtaining resources, and understanding one's social environment. Empowerment theory focuses on the positive rather than the negative. For example, the language of empowerment focuses on wellness as compared with illness, competence compared with deficits, and strength compared with weakness (Perkins & Zimmerman, 1995). Moreover, empowerment theory highlights capabilities, instead of risk factors, environmental influences as contrasted with views that blame the victim (Fetterman, 1981). A formal definition of empowerment is:

> an intentional ongoing process centered in the local community, involving mutual respect, critical reflection, caring, and group participation through which people lacking in equal share of valued resources gain greater access to and control over those resources. (Cornell Empowerment Group, 1989, p. 1)

This definition is in accord with a Freirean tradition in that people are required to take an active role in their own transformation and take action to gain greater control over their lives. Empowerment theory is divided into processes and outcomes. According to Zimmerman (2000):

---

[1] The culture of silence is designed to indoctrinate and condition people to think of themselves as useless, without value, and incapable of making a meaningful contribution to society.

> Empowerment processes are ones in which attempts to gain control, obtain
> needed resources, and critically understand one's social environment are fun-
> damental. The process is empowering if it helps people develop skills so they
> can become independent problem solvers and decision makers . . . Empower-
> ment outcomes refer to operationalization of empowerment so we can study
> the consequences of citizen attempts to gain greater control in their commu-
> nity or the effects of interventions designed to empower participants. (p. 3)

Empowerment theory helps operationalize both empowerment evaluation and Freirean pedagogy by separating out processes from outcomes.
Empowerment evaluation and Freirean pedagogy provide people with conceptual skills required to critically understand their social environment and
become independent problem solvers.

Self-Determination

This is one of the foundational concepts underlying empowerment theory.
Self-determination is defined as the ability to chart one's own course in life.
It consists of numerous interconnected capabilities, such as the ability to
identify and express needs; establish goals or expectations and a plan of action to achieve them; identify resources; make rational choices from various
alternative courses of action; take appropriate steps to pursue objectives;
evaluate short- and long-term results, including reassessing plans and expectations and taking necessary detours; and persist in the pursuit of those
goals. A breakdown at any juncture of this network of capabilities—as well
as various environmental factors—can reduce a person's likelihood of being
self-determined.[2]

These are instrumental microsteps required for people to accomplish
their objectives, build confidence, design new challenging goals, and ultimately take charge of their own lives. Freire recognized the need for people
to take action grounded in reality to transform their lives. These steps are a
blueprint for action on a microlevel.

Process Use

This represents much of the rationale or logic underlying empowerment
evaluation in practice, because it cultivates ownership by placing the approach in community and staff members' hands. The more that people are
engaged in conducting their own evaluations, the more likely they are to
believe in them, because the evaluation findings are theirs. In addition, a
byproduct of this experience is that they learn to think evaluatively. This
makes them more likely to make decisions and take actions based on their

---

[2] See also Bandura (1982) for more details on issues related to self-efficacy and self-
determination.

evaluation data. This way of thinking is at the heart of process use[3] (see Patton, 1997, 2005).

In an empowerment evaluation, thinking evaluatively is a product of guided immersion. This occurs when people conduct their own evaluation, assisted by an empowerment evaluator. Teaching people to think evaluatively is like teaching them to fish. It can last a lifetime and is what evaluative sustainability is all about—internalizing evaluation.

Empowerment evaluation models a Freirean liberating pedagogy in part because it recognizes the importance of people remaining in control of their own lives, instead of outside experts. As Freire (1974) warned: "the fact that investigators may in the first stage of the investigation approximately apprehend the complex of contradictions does not authorize them to begin to structure the program content of educational action. This perception of reality is still their own not that of the people" (p. 106).

Empowerment evaluation assumes people learn and internalize that learning from doing. Freire (1974) observed that it is only when people "become involved in the organized struggle for their liberation that they begin to believe in themselves" (p. 52). Moreover, people learn, become more fully conscious, and are liberated by conducting their own evaluations. Freire captured this self-reflective phenomenon when he explained that people's oppression itself needs to be the basis for reflection, which leads to the type and level of engagement required for liberation.

> This pedagogy makes oppression and its causes objects of reflection by the oppressed, and from that reflection will come their necessary engagement in the struggle for their liberation. And in the struggle this pedagogy will be made and remade. (p. 33)

A more fundamental concern is raised about people engaged in evaluating themselves—bias. For example, Scriven (1997), Stufflebeam (1995), and others have argued about the contaminating or biased nature of self-assessment.[4] However, Freire (1974) points out the flaw in that thinking:

> Some may think it inadvisable to include the people as investigators in the search for their own meaningful thematics: that their intrusive influence will "adulterate" the findings and thereby sacrifice the objectivity of the investigation. This view mistakenly presupposes that themes exist, in their original objective purity, outside men (and women)—as if these were things. Actually, themes exist in men (and women) in their relations with the world, with

---

[3] There is a substantial literature concerning the use of evaluation. However, most of it is devoted to lessons learned after the evaluation. The discussion of process use in this context focuses on use during an evaluation (see also Patton, 1997, 1998, 2005).
[4] See Fetterman (2001) and Fetterman and Wandersman (2005) for a more detailed response to this critique.

reference to concrete facts ... There is, therefore, a relation between the given objective fact, the perception men (and women) have of this fact, and the generative themes. (p. 97–98)

No pedagogy is truly liberating if it continues to treat people as "unfortunates" and offers models from those in power. People "must be their own example in the struggle" (p. 39). This is how conscientização[5] (or conscientization—"the process by which human beings participate critically in a transforming act"; Freire, 1985, p. 106) is achieved and people become free "to create and construct, to wonder, and to venture" (p. 55). (See also Fetterman & Wandersman, 2007, for a response to the role of bias.)

Capacity Building

Capacity building has been a driving force in empowerment evaluation since its inception (Fetterman, 1994; Fetterman, Kaftarian, & Wandersman, 1996). The evaluation capacity literature has coincided with and intersected with the empowerment evaluation. (For more information about evaluation capacity building, see Duffy & Wandersman, 2007; Taylor-Ritzler et al., 2013.)

Labin, Duffy, Meyers, Wandersman, and Lesesne (2013) conducted a research synthesis on the topic and define evaluation capacity building (ECB) as "an intentional process to increase individual motivation, knowledge, and skills, and to enhance a group or organization's ability to conduct or use evaluation" (p. 2). The assumption is that ECB strategies will improve individual attitudes, knowledge, and skills as evidenced by behavioral changes. In addition, ECB strategies will facilitate sustainable organizational learning.

Freire also believed in the capacity of ordinary citizens (literate or illiterate) to analyze their own reality, to "'re-consider' through the 'considerations' of others, their own previous 'consideration.'" The purpose of "individuals analyzing their own reality is to become aware of their prior, distorted perceptions, and thereby to have a new perception of that reality" (p. 114). Empowerment evaluation and Freirean practice use many of the same mechanisms or procedures to build a reflective, sustainable evaluative capacity and culture—placing the work in the hands of the people themselves (with guidance).

---

[5] Conscientização is a Brazilian word. It is the process by which people develop a critical consciousness about society and their role as a group in the world. It is generally discussed in terms of consciousness in the practice of liberation. However, the separation between consciousness and the world is artificial. It is a dialectical relationship between the two that makes conscientização possible. Separating them results in "illusions of idealism or mechanistic errors" (p. 106).

New Directions for Evaluation • DOI: 10.1002/ev

A Theory of Action

Finally, the alignment of *theories of use and action* explains how empowerment evaluation helps people produce desired results. The theory of use is usually the espoused operating theory about how a program or organization works. It is a useful tool, generally based on program personnel views. The theory of action is often compared with the theory of use. Theory of use is the actual program reality, the observable behavior of stakeholders (see Argyris & Schon, 1978). People engaged in empowerment evaluations create a theory of action at one stage and test it against the existing theory of use during a later stage. Similarly, they create a new theory of action as they plan for the future. Because empowerment evaluation is an ongoing and iterative process, stakeholders test their theories of action against theories in use to determine whether their strategies are being implemented as recommended or designed. The theories go hand in hand in empowerment evaluation.

Freire recommended dialogue and discussion, followed by action, and then reflection on practice again. In essence, he is suggesting a comparison of precisely these theories. (This approach is discussed in additional detail under cycles of reflection and action.) The juxtaposition of theories of use and action are the mechanisms by which people build their capacity to learn, and as Freire suggested, to adapt to the world, intervene, re-create, and transform it.

Principles

The theoretical foundations of empowerment evaluation lead to specific principles required to inform quality practice. Empowerment evaluation principles provide a sense of direction and purposefulness throughout an evaluation. Empowerment evaluation is guided by 10 specific principles (Fetterman & Wandersman, 2005, pp. 1–2, 27–41,42–72). They include:

1. Improvement—empowerment evaluation is designed to help people improve program performance; it is designed to help people build on their successes and re-evaluate areas meriting attention
2. Community ownership—empowerment evaluation values and facilitates community control; use and sustainability are dependent on a sense of ownership
3. Inclusion—empowerment evaluation invites involvement, participation, and diversity; contributions come from all levels and walks of life
4. Democratic participation—participation and decision making should be open and fair
5. Social justice—evaluation can and should be used to address social inequities in society

6. Community knowledge—empowerment evaluation respects and values community knowledge

7. Evidence-based strategies—empowerment evaluation respects and uses the knowledge base of scholars (in conjunction with community knowledge)

8. Capacity building—empowerment evaluation is designed to enhance stakeholders' ability to conduct evaluation and to improve program planning and implementation

9. Organizational learning—data should be used to evaluate new practices, inform decision making, and implement program practices; empowerment evaluation is used to help organizations learn from their experience (building on successes, learning from mistakes, and making midcourse corrections)

10. Accountability—empowerment evaluation is focused on outcomes and accountability; empowerment evaluations functions within the context of existing policies, standards, and measures of accountability; did the program or initiative accomplish its objectives?

Empowerment evaluation principles help evaluators and community members make decisions that are in alignment with the larger purpose or goals associated with capacity building and self-determination. The principle of inclusion, for example, reminds evaluators and community leaders to include rather than exclude members of the community, even though fiscal, logistic, and personality factors might suggest otherwise. The capacity-building principle reminds the evaluator to provide community members with the opportunity to collect their own data, even though it might initially be faster and easier for the evaluator to collect the same information. The accountability principle guides community members to hold one another accountable. It also situates the evaluation within the context of external requirements and credible results or outcomes (see Fetterman, 2005, p. 2).

These principles are in alignment with Freirean pedagogy. For example, the principles of community ownership, inclusion, and democratic decision making highlight the significance of community involvement and control. Community members are expected to authentically participate in, if not control, evaluation-related decision making, concerning issues that directly affect their lives. Empowerment evaluation and Freirean pedagogy are in agreement that the presence of people struggling "for their liberation will be what it should be: not pseudo-participation, but committed involvement" (p. 69). In addition, empowerment evaluation's commitment to social justice shares the same Freirean assumptions about the world, specifically, that there are inequities throughout the world and there is a pressing need to address them in a timely manner—through action. Accountability, for both empowerment evaluation and Freirean discourse, is paramount. It must be preceded by dialogue and understanding, but it is one of the best tests of effectiveness. Accountability, in this case, refers to both individual responsibility to the group and the group's responsibility to larger societal forces, including producing outcomes.

Concepts

Empowerment evaluation concepts provide a more instrumental view of how to implement the approach. Key concepts include cycles of reflection and action, communities of learners, and reflective practitioners (see Fetterman, Deitz, & Gesundheit, 2010).[6]

Cycles of Reflection and Action

This involves ongoing phases of analysis, decision making, and implementation (based on evaluation findings). It is a cyclical process. Programs are dynamic, not static, and require continual feedback as they change and evolve. Freire described the same process in the context of transformation (p. 36) and liberation, explaining "reflection—true reflection—leads to action. On the other hand, when the situation calls for action, that action will constitute an authentic praxis only if its consequences become the object of critical reflection" (p. 52–53).

Cycles of reflection and action are ongoing processes designed to contribute to long-term, sustainable forms of social change and transformation. It is this cyclical testing of ideas and strategies in practice (and revision based on feedback) in the real world that knowledge is gained. As Freire explains: "Knowledge emerges only through invention and re-invention, through the restless, impatient, continuing, hopeful inquiry human beings pursue in the world, with the world, and with each other" (p. 58).

Community of Learners

Empowerment evaluation is driven by a group process. It creates a community of learners. Members of the group learn from each other, serving as their own peer review group, critical friend, resource, and norming mechanism. Individual members of the group hold each other accountable concerning progress toward stated goals.

Freire was also committed to group learning and believed that real change could not be accomplished by the individual alone, but needed to be understood and accomplished through the group (pp. 34, 52, 88, 100). As Freire (1974) explained:

---

[6] These concepts are influenced by traditional organizational development and transformation theorists including Argyris and Schon (1978) and Senge (1994), as well as evaluators associated with organizational learning (Preskill & Torres, 1999).

I can not think for others or without others, nor can others think for me. Even if the people's thinking is superstitious or naive, it is only as they rethink their assumptions in action that they can change. Producing and acting upon their own ideas—not consuming those of others. (p. 100)

Reflective Practitioners

Finally, empowerment evaluations and Freirean pedagogy help create reflective practitioners. Reflective practitioners use data to inform their decisions and actions concerning their own daily activities. This produces a self-aware and self-actualized individual who has the capacity to apply this world-view to all aspects of their life. As individuals develop and enhance their own capacity, they improve the quality of the group's exchange, deliberation, and action plans.

A Lift Up

Empowerment evaluation and Freire's liberating educational approach help raise consciousness and encourage people to take responsibility for their own lives. They help people engage in cycles of reflection and action in order to become more critically aware of their existence, take steps to improve their performance as members of a group, and contribute to their community's development. These approaches help lift people up, instead of pushing them down (see also Lentz et al., 2005).

Generative Themes

The process of engaging in empowerment evaluation generates priorities for inquiry that are similar to what Freire referred to as "generative themes." Without these generative themes, critical topics and issues may never be made explicit and thus never grappled with. Freire observed that these

themes may or may not be perceived in their true significance. They may simply be felt—sometimes not even that. But the nonexistence of themes within the sub-units is absolutely impossible. The fact that individuals in a certain area do not perceive a generative theme, or perceive it in a distorted way, may only reveal a limit-situation . . . in which men (and women) are still submerged. (p. 94)

Generative themes provide the relevant substance for active engagement—the things people are most concerned about. This sets the stage for one of the most important parts of the process—authentic dialogue. Similar to Freirean pedagogy, through dialogue, existing thoughts will change and new knowledge will be created.

NEW DIRECTIONS FOR EVALUATION • DOI: 10.1002/ev

Dialogue

The dialogue about priorities is one of the most important parts of the empowerment evaluation process. In addition to clarifying issues, evidence is used to support viewpoints and "sacred cows" are surfaced and examined during dialogue. Moreover, the process of specifying the reason or evidence for a priority provides the group with a more efficient and focused manner of identifying what needs to be done next, during the planning for the future step of the process. Instead of generating an unwieldy list of strategies and solutions that may or may not be relevant to the issues at hand, the group can focus its energies on the specific concerns and reasons for a low priority rating that were raised in the dialogue or exchange.

The dialogue is analytical and often emotional. Empowerment evaluation has responded to critiques focused on an objectivist perspective without sufficient attention to emotion (Fetterman, 1995, 2001; Stufflebeam, 1995). Freire recognized the dialectical nature of these human features. On the one hand, Freire highlighted the value of "objectively verifiable" (p. 35) data. However, he also observed: "One cannot conceive of objectivity without subjectivity" (p. 35). The subjective and the objective are in a "constant dialectical relationship" (p. 35). Freire referred to this as "reason soaked with emotion."

Empowerment evaluation embraces this combination. People have emotions. Emotions are a powerful force shaping people's consciousness and action. According to Freire, "To deny the importance of subjectivity in the process of transforming the world and history is naïve and simplistic" (p. 35).[7] The level of emotion in an exchange is often a test of the depth of the issues confronted. However, reality must be confronted by a combination of the analytical and the emotional.

> A mere perception of reality not followed by this critical intervention (objectifying and acting upon that reality) will not lead to a transformation of objective reality—precisely because it is not a true perception. This is the case of a purely subjectivist perception by someone who forsakes objective reality and creates a false substitute. (p. 37)

Dialogue is a critical part of the pedagogy of critical consciousness or *conscientização*. People confront each other with an evaluative view of the functionality, productivity, and adaptability of their community and where it is situated in the larger society. They create meaning by sharing their view of reality with each other and coming to a consensus about the world they

---

[7] "The separation of objectivity from subjectivity, the denial of the latter when analyzing reality or acting upon it, is objectivism" (Freire, p. 35). This denies the counterbalancing influence of subjectivity and emotions. This explains much about the initial debates between Fetterman (1995), who includes emotions in the human equation, and Stufflebeam (1994), who argued for an objectivist approach to evaluation.

live in and what needs to be done next to improve their lives. This is often where the "elephant" in the room emerges; the underlying problem or inequity that everyone knows about, but no one is willing to surface and discuss in daily life. The dialogue moves the group beyond needs to causes and links that to their perceived needs. Logic models and theories of change (without the jargon or terminology) become more meaningful and useful. Critical dialogue contributes to critical consciousness. Reflection based on a critical dialogue propels groups into action. According to Freire: "critical dialogue presupposes action." Planning for the future, in empowerment evaluation, is built on the critical dialogue or taking stock exchanges. It represents the coconstructed road map (or intervention) required to accomplish community goals.

Planning for the Future

Many evaluations conclude at the taking-stock phase. However, taking stock is a baseline and a launching-off point for the rest of the empowerment evaluation. After rating and discussing programmatic activities, it is important to do something about the findings. It is time to plan for the future. This involves generating goals, strategies, and credible evidence (to determine if the strategies are being implemented and if they are effective). The goals are directly related to the activities selected in the taking-stock step. Planning for the future can only be conducted after the group has taken stock of their situation. In other words, their plan of action, similar to Freirean steps, comes after dialogue (taking stock). In addition, taking stock is preceded by an initial discussion about the group's purpose or mission. This provides an intellectual coherence to the endeavor and like Freire, provides an internal theory guiding practice and action. However, raising consciousness, implementing action plans, and testing hypotheses require monitoring if the initiatives are to produce desired outcomes (and remain on track and timely).

Monitoring the Strategies

Many programs, projects, and evaluations fail at this stage for lack of individual and group accountability. Individuals who spoke eloquently and/or emotionally about a certain topic during the early steps of the empowerment evaluation are asked to volunteer to lead specific task forces to respond to identified problems or concerns. They do not have to complete the task. However, they are responsible for taking the lead in a circumscribed area (a specific goal) and reporting the status of the effort periodically at ongoing management meetings. Similarly, the community members make a commitment to reviewing the status of these new strategies as a group (making midcourse corrections if the strategies are not working). Conventional and innovative evaluation tools are used to monitor the strategies. An evaluation dashboard is a particularly useful tool to monitor change or progress over time. It consists of baselines, benchmarks or milestones, goals, and actual performance. Metrics enable community members to compare, for example, their baseline assessments with their benchmarks/milestones or expected points of progress, actual performance, and goals. This approach is aligned with Freirean pedagogy because it places the tools to monitor performance in the hands of the people in the community. It is transparent, enabling staff and community members to monitor their own performance, while allowing sponsors to determine if additional assistance is needed along the way. It is also a tool to build evaluation capacity because it teaches people how to monitor their own performance, learning in time to make adjustments in a timely fashion.

Role

Relationships play a pivotal role in the process of conducting an empowerment evaluation. The role of the critical friend[8] merits attention because it is like a fulcrum in terms of fundamental relationships. Applied improperly, it can be like a wedge inhibiting movement and change; applied correctly, this role can be used to leverage and maximize the potential of a group.

Empowerment evaluators have considerable expertise, but as critical friends or coaches, they help keep the evaluation systematic, rigorous, and on track. They are able to function in this capacity by advising, rather than directing or controlling, an evaluation. They provide a structure or set of steps to conduct an evaluation. They recommend, rather than require, specific activities and tools. They listen and rely on the group's knowledge and understanding of their local situation.

The empowerment evaluator differs from many traditional evaluators. Instead of being the "expert" and completely independent, separate, and detached from the people they work with, so as not to get "contaminated" or "biased," the empowerment evaluator works closely with and alongside program staff members and participants.

This approach is aligned with Freirean pedagogy, in which the leader works closely with the community, not as an outside expert distant from the community. In both approaches, the evaluator or facilitator refrains from assuming control, framing the discussion, dominating the dialogue, or prescribing action plans. Instead, the group takes the lead and works together as a group. Freire draws a similar picture of the role in his comparison of teachers and students[9]:

---

[8] These concepts are influenced by traditional organizational development and transformation theorists including Argyris and Schon (1978) and Senge (1994), as well as evaluators associated with organizational learning (Preskill & Torres, 1999).
[9] According to Freire, the "teacher is no longer merely the one who teaches, but one who is himself taught in dialogue with the students, who in turn while being taught also teach" (p. 67).

Teachers and students (leadership and people), co-intent on reality are both Subjects, not only in the task of unveiling that reality and thereby coming to know it critically, but in the task of re-creating that knowledge. As they attain this knowledge of reality through common reflection and action, they discover themselves as its permanent re-creators. (p. 56)

The Freirean facilitator and empowerment evaluator both serve the group or community in an attempt to help them maximize their potential and unleash their creative and productive energy for a common good. Important attributes of a critical friend include creating an environment conductive to dialogue and discussion; providing or requesting data to inform decision making; facilitating rather than leading; and being open to ideas, inclusive, and willing to learn (see Fetterman, 2009; Fetterman et al., 2010, for additional details of this role).

Conclusion

Empowerment evaluation and Freirean pedagogy are aligned in both theory and practice. The alignment is most pronounced with transformative empowerment evaluation. However, both streams of empowerment evaluation embrace essential features, including critical thinking, authentic dialogue, conscientização, and action. Empowerment evaluation and Freirean pedagogy are emancipatory, and if applied appropriately, help people free themselves from the constraints placed on them, as well as the limitations they place on themselves. Together, they can also help to transform the practice of evaluation.

References

Argyris, C., & Schon, D. A. (1978). *Organizational learning: A theory of action perspective.* Reading, MA: Addison-Wesley.

Bandura, A. (1982). Self-efficacy mechanism in human agency. *American psychologist, 37*(2), 122.

Chinman, M., Imm, P., & Wandersman, A. (2004). *Getting to outcomes: Promoting accountability through methods and tools for planning, implementation, and evaluation.* Santa Monica, CA: RAND Corporation. Retrieved from http://www.rand.org/pubs/technical_reports/TR101/

Cornell Empowerment Group. (1989). Empowerment and family support. *Networking Bulletin, 1*, 1–23.

Duffy, J. L., & Wandersman, A. (2007, November). *A review of research on evaluation capacity building strategies.* Paper presented at the annual conference of the American Evaluation Association, Baltimore, MD.

Fetterman, D. M. (1981). Blaming the victim: The problem of evaluation design and federal involvement, and reinforcing world views in education. *Human Organization, 40*, 67–77.

Fetterman, D. M. (1994). Empowerment evaluation. *Evaluation Practice, 15*(1), 1–15.

Fetterman, D. M. (1995). Response to Dr. Daniel Stufflebeam's Empowerment Evaluation, objectivist evaluation, and evaluation standards: Where the future of evaluation should not go, where it needs to go, October 1994, 321–338. *American Journal of Evaluation, 16,* 179–199.

Fetterman, D. M. (2001). *Foundations of empowerment evaluation.* Thousand Oaks, CA: Sage.

Fetterman, D. M. (2005). A window into the heart and soul of empowerment evaluation. In D. M. Fetterman & A. Wandersman (Eds.), *Empowerment evaluation principles in practice.* New York, NY: Guilford Press.

Fetterman, D. M. (2009). Empowerment evaluation at the Stanford University School of Medicine: Using a critical friend to improve the clerkship experience. *Ensaio: Avaliação e Políticas Públicas em Educação, 17*(63), 197–204.

Fetterman, D. M. (2015). Empowerment evaluation and action research: A convergence of values, principles, and purpose. In H. Bradbury (Ed.), *The SAGE Handbook of Action Research.* Thousand Oaks, CA: Sage.

Fetterman, D. M., Deitz, J., & Gesundheit, N. (2010). Empowerment evaluation: A collaborative approach to evaluating and transforming a medical school curriculum. *Academic Medicine, 85*(5), 813–820.

Fetterman, D. M., Kaftarian, S. J., & Wandersman, A. (1996). *Empowerment evaluation: Knowledge and tools for self-assessment and accountability.* Thousand Oaks, CA: Sage.

Fetterman, D. M., Rodriguez-Campos, L., Wandersman, A., & Goldfarb O'Sullivan, R. (2014). Collaborative, participatory, and empowerment evaluation: Building a strong foundation for stakeholder involvement approaches to evaluation (a response to Cousins, Whitmore, and Shulha). *American Journal of Evaluation, 35*(1), 144–148.

Fetterman, D. M., & Wandersman, A. (2005). *Empowerment evaluation principles in practice.* New York, NY: Guilford Press.

Fetterman, D. M., & Wandersman, A. (2007). Empowerment evaluation: yesterday, today, and tomorrow. *American Journal of Evaluation, 28*(2):179–198.

Freire, P. (1974). *Pedagogy of the oppressed.* New York, NY: Seabury Press.

Freire, P. (1985). *The politics of education: Culture, power, and liberation.* Granby, MA: Bergin and Garvey.

Labin, S., Duffy, J. L., Meyers, D. C., Wandersman, A., & Lesesne, C. A. (2013). A research synthesis of the evaluation capacity building literature. *American Journal of Evaluation, 33*(3), 307–338.

Lentz, B. E., Imm, P. S., Yost, J. B., Johnson, N. P., Barron, C., Lindberg, M. S., et al. (2005). Empowerment evaluation and organizational learning: A case study of a community coalition designed to prevent chid abuse and neglect. In D. M. Fetterman & A. Wandersman (Eds.), *Empowerment evaluation principles in practice* (pp. 155–183). Thousand Oaks, CA: Sage.

Patton M. Q. (1997). *Utilization-focused evaluation.* Thousand Oaks, CA: Sage.

Patton, M. Q. (1998). Discovering process use. *Evaluation, 4*(2), 225–233.

Patton, M. Q. (2005). Toward distinguishing empowerment evaluation and placing it in a larger context; take two. *American Journal of Evaluation, 26,* 408–414.

Perkins, D., & Zimmerman, M. (1995). Empowerment theory, research, and application. *American Journal of Community Psychology, 23*(5), 569–579.

Preskill, H., & Torres, R. (1999). *Evaluative inquiry for learning in organizations.* Thousand Oaks, CA: Sage.

Scriven, M. (1997). Empowerment evaluation examined. *Evaluation Practice, 18*(2), 165–175.

Senge, P. (1994). *The fifth discipline: The art and practice of the learning organization.* New York, NY: Doubleday.

Shaull, R. (1974). Foreword. In P. Freire (Ed.), *Pedagogy of the oppressed.* New York, NY: Seabury Press.

Stufflebeam, D. (1994). Empowerment evaluation, objectivist evaluation, and evaluation standards: Where the future of evaluation should not go, where it needs to go. *Evaluation Practice, 15*(3), 321–338.

Taylor-Ritzler, T., Suarez-Balcazar, Y., Garcia-Iriarte, E., Henry, D., & Balcazar, F. (2013). Understanding and measuring evaluation capacity: A model and instrument validation study. *American Journal of Evaluation, 34*, 190–206.

Wandersman, A., & Snell-Johns, J. (2005). Empowerment evaluation: Clarity, dialogue, and growth. *American Journal of evaluation, 26*(3), 421–428.

Zimmerman, M. (2000). Empowerment theory. In J. Rappaport & E. Seidman (Eds.), *Handbook of community psychology* (pp. 2–45). New York, NY: Kluwer Academic/Plenum.

DAVID M. FETTERMAN, *Stanford University Ph.D., is President and CEO of Fetterman & Associates, an international evaluation consulting firm. He is also a faculty member at the University of Charleston and San Jose State University. He introduced empowerment evaluation to the field during his tenure as president of the American Evaluation Association.*

New Directions for Evaluation • DOI: 10.1002/ev

INDEX

NEW DIRECTIONS FOR EVALUATION

ORDER FORM SUBSCRIPTION AND SINGLE ISSUES

DISCOUNTED BACK ISSUES:

Use this form to receive 20% off all back issues of *New Directions for Evaluation*.
All single issues priced at **$23.20** (normally $29.00)

TITLE	ISSUE NO.	ISBN

Call 1-800-835-6770 or see mailing instructions below. When calling, mention the promotional code JBNND to receive your discount. For a complete list of issues, please visit www.wiley.com/WileyCDA/WileyTitle/productCd-EV.html

SUBSCRIPTIONS: (1 YEAR, 4 ISSUES)

☐ New Order ☐ Renewal

U.S.	☐ Individual: $89	☐ Institutional: $380
CANADA/MEXICO	☐ Individual: $89	☐ Institutional: $422
ALL OTHERS	☐ Individual: $113	☐ Institutional: $458

Call 1-800-835-6770 or see mailing and pricing instructions below.
Online subscriptions are available at www.onlinelibrary.wiley.com

ORDER TOTALS:

Issue / Subscription Amount: $ _____

Shipping Amount: $ _____
(for single issues only – subscription prices include shipping)

Total Amount: $ _____

SHIPPING CHARGES:

First Item $6.00
Each Add'l Item $2.00

(No sales tax for U.S. subscriptions. Canadian residents, add GST for subscription orders. Individual rate subscriptions must be paid by personal check or credit card. Individual rate subscriptions may not be resold as library copies.)

BILLING & SHIPPING INFORMATION:

☐ **PAYMENT ENCLOSED:** *(U.S. check or money order only. All payments must be in U.S. dollars.)*

☐ **CREDIT CARD:** ☐ VISA ☐ MC ☐ AMEX

Card number _____Exp. Date_____

Card Holder Name_____Card Issue #_____

Signature _____Day Phone_____

☐ **BILL ME:** *(U.S. institutional orders only. Purchase order required.)*

Purchase order # _____
　　　　　　　　Federal Tax ID 13559302 • GST 89102-8052

Name_____

Address_____

Phone_____ E-mail_____

Copy or detach page and send to:　**John Wiley & Sons, Inc. / Jossey Bass**
PO Box 55381
Boston, MA 02205-9850

PROMO JBNND